LIFE
AT THE
BOTTOM
OF THE
WORLD

By

Red Jordan Arobateau

LIFE AT THE BOTTOM OF THE WORLD

Journal #19 in the Journey Series

Any resemblance to any person living or dead is purely coincidental.

All un-attributed quotes are from the Prophet Red Jordan Arobateau.

Cover Sketch of the Artist-Author by Baz Wenwei Chua

ISBN: 978-1-300-81873-1

Published by RED JORDAN PRESS
Redjordanarobateau.com
USA

Part- 1

Well you are going to want, to really really really want to get away from it. All thru the bible Jesus is forever getting away from the multitude—going away in boats, going up on mountain tops, trying to have private moments to heal himself.

Jesus H. Christ. Just thought—there has been 2 suicides in our community in the last 6 months. Both horrible...

Paul—jumped in front of moving subway train. Christophe Lee—Hung himself.

Hideous hideous, hideous! The persistent stink coming from somewhere around my bed has been traced! Have been very clean, and changed bed sheets just yesterday—the stink persisted.

It must be a mouse Penny half killed and it crept away to die and is rotting somewhere...

Foolish foolish fool! Finally after suffering thru a week of stink, saw Penny slink under bed and making mysterious moves.

The OM painfully bent down on hands/knees, shone his flashlight under the bed—it was mounds of shit! Cat Shit under his bed!

ARUUURURGHHHGGG!

To conserve energy OM had been closing bathroom door to just a cat-size space so the heat would fully stay in the rest of his small studio—the bathroom was perpetually cold. Nobody would mind that! They aren't in the bathroom that long! Or are they.... Evidently Cat did not want to go into cold bathroom, and also associating bathroom w/her water torture—life saving kidney dialyses treatment—also being locked in for several hours when parrots flew about. So she began to shit under the bed, also to pee—and this in the most difficult part of the bed to access!!!!!!!!

ARRRRRRRRUGGGH!

Had to painfully crawl under bed w/paper towels and disinfectant and clean to the best of my ability. Now the bathroom door will remain open. Wide Open. Fuck Shit.

T-woman on bus that he knew; was very obnoxious. W/no regard for others she sits in the handicapped section—for old & disabled. 3 old people on canes & in walkers climbed aboard bus--when asked to relinquish her seat to someone visibly crippled, she yells: *I'm disabled!* And was busy yaking on her cellphone. Others dismiss this way of behavior—they recognize by her mannerisms and voice timber she is transsexual—so: *oh, that person is crazy—leave them alone.* This new girl is soon to have her lower surgery, thax to trans health care advocates in the city—what a relief! What torture our trans oldsters had to endure before it! I hope some of the old gals—and guys will be able to access what the new ones are now receiving. Even top surgery is beginning to be covered—15 years after I paid for my own, out of a fortuitous windfall of money...

More news about today's topic. Now can you help counsel a troubled veteran of the Iraqi war by taking him to the rifle range! Duahh! This is where one of US military's Ace snipers met his fate—a discharged soldier turned on him & fired point blank, killing the hero & one other man. I would think the counseling would involve a peaceful atmosphere w/no shell shocking gunfire!

Bang of hammers. 2nd story rises. Old & poor left behind.

His therapist talked about the use of the word tranny—for which he'd been trashed and insulted in that non-supportive FTM group:

> Back in the earlier times there was no discussion of transsexuals at all—it was the word that dared not speak its name. Nothing ever mentioned about transsexuals. So for the first time people began to take the word tranny and use it for themselves and it was a community term uniting us—so now this new generation has come along and they don't have any of this history. They speak out of their small experience and don't understand where any of it is coming from.

Christopher Lee is dead, he started the Tranny Film Festival —none of them attended the memorial, none of them even knew who he was.

Am @ Trans Space for the first time in months as you can see by my journal entries—not there, but down hall @ health clinic—for blood panels.

Saw wonderful trans gals there who I remember have been warm to me—numerous hugs and shouts of joy to see me! (Even tho she is not passable.) So what is the other ones excuse?

Anyway glad to see these gals. Got $5 gift certificate for filling out one of endless surveys.

2 high tek women in glittery pants suits stride along Van Ness Ave, speaking of stem cell research and the brain & 15 years ago the stupid then-president vetoed stem cell research probably not out of his personal beliefs—but to milk votes out of ignorant southern bigots masked in religiosity;-- meanwhile all the intelligenzia was fleeing our nation to continue their research on stem cells in foreign lands of more intelligence.

PM
Of course after he'd been up @ Trans Space & seen some of his old tranny gal pals, the OM immediately felt embarashed by saying how he never wanted to spend any time w/any of them again—after dealing with the hideous one @ Coyote. He was truly glad to see these new women. (Some of them older…)

The empty places.

The Chinese have come on TV essentially saying what I said yesterday. The Chinese embraced the rise of the middle class from the start, where as the rise of the middle class in medieval Europe was opposed by the royalty and by the church who tried to hold them down—which is essentially why the middle class eventually overthrew these institutions.

W/3 of the old gay men discussed Chinese birth signs—year of the snake, dragon, etc:

6

The year of the peter.

When I was in my teens, 18, 19, running w/an older crowd who worked and drank off-hours, drinking to excess; partying non-stop, I decided sleeping was a waste of time! 8 whole hours asleep could be used far better in hanging out w/friends, partying, carrying on conversations, having fun; going, going. Going 24 hours until I realized into the 3rd day w/no sleep I was grinding like a groundout wheel, my eyes falling closed every minute and literally could not force myself to go on any further without sleep.

As a worker I found, when scheduling myself to a job 25 to 30 hours a week, it was the barest necessity to pay bills, and still allowed me an edge of time to create—if I did not sleep more then 5 hours a night. A good 5 hours of work. So I went on year after year sleeping only 5 hours a night on 5 day work weeks, and only catching up to a full 8 to 10 hours on my weekend.

At some point in my 60's, once retired I realized how I hated the feeling of not having had enough sleep @ night—the whole day dragging myself forward, coffee upon coffee, and what torture it was, if I'd only got 4 or 5 hours of sleep the night before, what hellified torture to stay awake the next day!

We become beautiful in God. We are evil, but God shines into us, and if we welcome God into our minds and hearts we become beautiful w/ the presence of God.

Thursday, February 14
Another piece of furniture defaced by spoiled young hipster punks from affluence, leaning against a building by the side of the road; surface of this nice table marred by graffiti—they have no idea a poorer person may have wanted to take it for their humble home; material goods mean nothing to the spoiled young punks who have grown up w/plenty! This table might have graced the single room of some SRO dweller. Die hipster spoiled punks.

One abandon sock in the corridor of the mosque. Lost in rush for the Call to Worship.

Well our ancient ancestors who lived in caves/trees could not imagine being in trouble finding a place to go to the toilet. They went outside and peed anywhere. They shat in special areas away from camp. Today all this concrete, eyes watching—it is such a problem

WallGrims God I hate these people taking money out of my pocket. Another On Sale scam, which is not really a savings.

All my friends are busy right now; Baz w/his house—caretaking; Dr. Sam w/his new house; Jasmin w/her show w/Veronica Combs dancer turned chanteuse!

Talked to Jolly Olde Pervert— shared a laugh or two about sex & cruised men's crotches & Transman who was bisexual saw one buxom beauty accompanied by her boy pal, & commented on such to which the Olde Jolly responds: *You take her, leave him to me.*

> I almost died! I got hit by a BMW.
> --Blax homeless man/w naps.

> ***

> Of course I get young men—there's no men left older then me!
> There's no one near my age!
> --Olde Pervert

PM
I am laying here smelling stinking cat shit under my bed.

Did I tell you found the source of this hideous stench—the cat had resorted to shitting under the bed—using it as a cat box—because was keeping the bathroom door partially closed & it became frigid in there, since no heat could get in.

I have opened the bathroom door forever.

Put boards up around the bed so cat can't get under there.

Am too tired to clean up any more of the shit that remains under bed. Will wait until it stinks itself out and becomes fossilized.

One can see by my journals that I have been plagued by:

> Dust mites
> Cat stinking shit under my bed
> Hawk attack
> No money but rent due

The plagues of Pharaoh!

Illinois, 9th state to pass gay marriage! My state! Which drove me out w/its unfair on-the-take vice cop raids on our bars due to Mayor Daly catholic bigoted racist anti-gay corrupt politician.

Add to lists of insults, selfish money hoarding immigrant w/good jobs but who crowd 5 children & 3 adults into one tiny room—sharp impact on ceiling.

Friday, February 14
Found bread & shrimp on top of newspaper rack on street—whisked bread into his pack—left shrimp—it might be spoiled, which is the nature of fish, which doesn't stand up well.

When Transman entered the computer place he saw his & Jasmin's ex-roomate there, also using the free facility. He had sat next to her but 5 minutes (the only other space of 4) when she told him to kindly close down the audio on his computer, it must have bothered her:

> Please turn your volume off on the audio.

> I don't have any audio on my computer.

> You can turn it down on your computer.

> There is no audio on my computer! You must be hearing something coming from somewhere else!

At this point the ex-roommate turned to the African American woman across from her:

> Please turn off the volume on your audio.

9

I don't have any volume on my computer!

I don't have any volume on my computer—but I can hear
something—I think it's coming *from your own computer!*

Sure enough. The watchful presence of the nice people at the Center
came over and informed her, sadly, it was her own damn computer
making the noise—she having accused 2 of us of being the ones at
fault!

Snap! She turned off her damn computer without further comment.

Ring Card Girl—name of person who holds up those cards between
rounds of prize fight—they are always ultra feminine; bare legged and
bare armed, walking about on the tallest glittery high heel pumps she
can manage—sex symbol, the prize to be fought for by the brawny
punchy brawlers swinging knock-out blows.

Oh, I have lost control of my yahoo email—all this deluge of
unwanted crap/and non-crap—but just don't have time to read it!
Need help! Maybe my delete button...

This is a new foreign-movie series on TV with grand publicity—
featuring an Anglo priest in Italy; it is a decent show and has a
love/God message—featuring this priest and his higher wisdom, his
gentle ways. It is a great statement—despite all the Fathers, He's, and
sexist patriarchal description of the Almighty. Oh but one bad part—
it has almost no women! Well the Priest will not have a female
companion/lover like the other detective series. It has a cast of 7 men
and one boy! This kid couldn't even have been a girl!

Oh, 2 females are in it, but they are written out of power—not the
power a glamorous leading lady, or a strong dowager would
command. They are a joke. Both roles are easy to dismiss—one
woman hysterical, half crazy or stupid, the other too old. No one will
take these women seriously. This is a bad milieu for a feminist to
immerse herself/himself week after week.

10

Got here & the ugly acting Mean One & her small entourage was occupying a table in the parklett. Henny was among them. All the tables and chairs outside were taken in this new clement weather after the long cold sunless months. But the OM had been walking outside quite a while so it was OK to be inside @ his window seat.

Why is Hawk always out here all of a sudden? —When he should be @ work? Vacation? Stay-cation?

Coyote.

One of the old gay men, in a plaid shirt & trousers, a very big replica of me—meaning big fat gut like me—rises slowly while leaning against outer cement wall of the café for support. Once fully standing, his knees locked into place, he stands for a full 5 minutes to regulate his blood pressure. Then forages across the street to his car.

We are all wearing out & slowing down.

Oh how the Old Man would love to be sizes smaller—his new trousers Jasmin bought 3 years ago were wearing out, w/tears @ the pocket & waistband—and 4 pairs unused new trousers—Dalora's hand-me downs—when they lost enormous weight—would fit him. They sat in a row in closet; brown, black, tan—waiting.

Across street a big bozo in rough clothes, worn blue jeans, ragged, with holes, he is walking on the cuffs—, dead shoes; hoody, stained; long unkempt hair; his bragging voice; speaks vehemently with an older man—he is a bozo, a bum; he will come to nothing—drowning in strong drink. But a few—a very few out of this type are somebody & will come to something... they're artists—dedicated to their craft, putting in 10, 12, hours a day in pursuit of capturing beauty. Painting it, describing it, singing lyrics to it. Welding unwieldy mobiles w/a blowtorch to it. Creating some message for the human species.

He is staggering smoking crashing up against golden flowerpots, brick walls of buildings—hollering; perpetually disappointed.

Often I write thru a Caucasian lens because that's the culture we are immersed in—hence some of my plays are white-dominated.

11

Saw his across-the-hall gay neighbor:

> Well the horrible day is here—laundry day.

> Well its not going to do itself is it?

Poor & strange-looking blax man sitting in Laundromat beside the long row of washing & drying machines; he is watching the TV, drinking sodas from the machine; must keep eye on him. He is apparently not here to do laundry, but passing time as one would in an arcade. Is he a thief—or simply an innocent victim of typecasting: *blax man in Laundromat up to no to good!*

PM
I can't believe this goddamn fucken' cat. Boarded up all 3 sides of the bed so she couldn't go down under it & shit/piss—left one small opening which was hard to board up. Now just saw her run out from under there—leaving a trail of wet cat paws, indicating she has not only gone under the bed –thru this small clumsy opening– but has pissed too!

Boarded it up w/piece of cardboard. Now it is done. Just to wait until the shit dies & decays and I can sweep it out.

Am so exhausted.

Myself, a global asset.

Last night a meteor crashed to earth in Russia at hypersonic speed of 160 thousand miles per hour. 1,000 Russians were hurt, and much damage done, but no deaths, thank God.

Saturday, February 16
OM trudged up street; he so fat, he so poor. On wai to meet Bro Leo. —Mess of students hover around Sutter Street the Art Academy; a suit comes past snaps photos of building entrance for some real-estate hi-finance corrupt deal.

We started out as hunter gatherers; men and men types went out in pursuit of meat—game; women and women types stayed close to

12

camp gathering nuts, roots, fruits, edible leaves; brought back water in gourds & skins; everyone in the small tribe ate. As civilizing progressed the tribes became too large and their weaker, less able members fell down into the lowest class in the worst poverty. The superfluous poor —well not superfluous because the middle class needs somebody to walk on.

Oh, Leo unraveled the mystery of the lotto to him. Told this black Jewish brother how Hashem had vividly instructed me while davaning in shul—orthodox— in Hebrew, before the bema, it was evil for me to cogitate over potential winning numbers, so when played the TX, I was always letting the machine pick it---thus making it possible for God to choose the numbers for me; not worrying, and fretting over it and doing mathematical calculations over it myself, which is a form of worship in itself. But Leo declared brilliantly that I must go further if this was the case, and instead of mediating over potential wining numbers—sin, as shown to me—I should meditate on *Hashem giving me the wining numbers* and pray and davan on this account, not just go up slap down a dollar on the store counter declaring: *let the machine play it!*

So, next Wednesday this is what I intend to do, and cast up prayers on this subject way head of time.

It was funny; as they walked, the OM complained about being so fat & struggling w/diet, and complained he'd had no breakfast, and little to eat the day before, and said:

>Is yogurt fattening?

>It depends on what kind it is. Pina Colada? Chocolate w/almonds?

>Vanilla.

>That's ok.

>I ate a big one tho. The 32 oz. But its all I'd eaten all day.

>That's ok then.

>And I had a pack of cheese... and some bread I found...

13

Well let the cheese stay in the store next time; don't bring the cheese home.

But its all I had... that and ground beef...

Oh... how much ground beef?

I cooked two packages—2 pounds but I only ate some of it...

Half?

No a quarter or less... And some cottage cheese...

Ah, well that should be ok...

And some frozen vegetables—peas & carrots....

Well by the end of his remembrance of the night before it turned out OM had had quite a bit to eat after all....

> Red: its such a relief going onto this other territory—men. I was getting so nowhere w/women. Women are so much more difficult then men. Harder to find... harder to get... They say some glamorous women are high maintenance femmes... but even the plain ones who aren't glamorous are a lot of work, a lot of trouble, and you can't get them either...

> All women are difficult. A woman is high maintenance. Period.
> --Leo

A funny was shared by the two friends, as Leo mentioned the recent brisk of a wonderful queer couple—a couple of queers! And Red inquired as to the genetic linage of the child:

> Is it their child—completely, did they use each other's parts—or did they get an egg donor, or a sperm donor?

> They got a surrogate.

> A surrogate egg donor, or just a surrogate mother?

14

I don't know all the cellular details!

@ the end of their evening as Bro Leo was going, in come two hipster artist friends Aaron Lawrence & Paul Kozen—Paul visiting from Seattle. Both are fine artists. They sat & chatted. Aaron said another crony, ----, who was now gone back to live w/family, having to recuperate w/going overboard on dope/drink—all of us mad artists. Red told the two how Alan Kaufman is putting thru a proposal to NY publishing house for his Outlaw Book Of Painters—in which we would all be featured. We spoke of going in establishments and seeing D Young V's work everywhere—and its like saying David Young has been here. *We are in Young territory* says Aaron. And Red mentioned Aaron's coup as having painted so much of the coffee shop on Pine Street down from Grace Cathedral—having done all the upstairs walls—DVYoung having done one wall over the bathroom. Aaron says he is going back there to do the tabletops—and laminate them.

PM
As I have progressed through my life—have seen many of my people drop off along the way. Dead. Dead when I was a young teen. Dead, when me in my 20's. And on, so that now, nearly 70's have seen 2 others dead—suicide over the last 6 months. They drop off.

I am going to say something which information received 3 days ago and forgot to write down. It concerns an unspeakable act committed by an Arab cleric of the highest standing in Iran. First I must say, privately I believe this story or rumor has a chance of being 80% false. So much bad information is coming out of the Middle East— information based on habits, customs which are correct and true— so that it is easy for some hot-head driven wild w/anger start right from a launching place of these actual truths to go on to invent utter lies— just to make a point, so what I am about to say, an unspeakable act, might not be true whatsoever.

Well the story is about a high-ranking Ayatollah, the highest on their religion—like our Pope (Ugh). It is said this Ayatollah went to visit one of his clans members of high rank, and there as a gift for the night he was given a 4 year old girl for his sexual pleasure. It is said the

15

cries of pain could be heard throughout the tent. He fucked her in the front hole & in the back.

Now if this is true it is unspeakable. If it is false, it is mimicking actual practices in that part of the world. Unspeakable!

Race really is a mental illness for some of us. Light—but not light enough. (Passá blanca). Black & always black—unchangeable.

Sunday, February 17
Life @ the bottom of the world. These words came to him upon awakening. The OM wrote them down thinking*: maybe this would be a good title for my next Journal.*

He headed out to class.

Martyr meaning witness. In the Catholic Church are designated red martyrs and white martyrs. One dies a bloody red death for the sake of God. The other a leads a life of daily death for God. Of denying self. Of seeking justice & truth despite the pain caused to self. Stuff like that. If any clerics wish to footnote my writings in the future for greater information to the readers they should do so speedily!

The geyser gushed jubilantly on the plaza; its base was silver-gold light.

A merry dog scooted across the plaza & went wee-wee against a garbage receptacle. Followed by a load-baring Chinese. —Baring Dog Toys!

Again—the question comes up to serve, to be active not only learning the Word, but taking it in and performing service—going further in service.

Gothic, cool, stately—few chairs tonight—only 2 in each of 4 corners. We assemble near the entrance by the baptismal font.

We spoke of martyrdom. Our Sound Is The Word—by Lucy Winkett.

Again the question—we have been trained here in the church by many lessons over, and over & over & over each Sunday instructed—*what next step will you make?*

Some people sit in church Sunday after Sunday after Sunday, decade upon decade, 40, 50, 60, years—they hear the working of miracles by Jesus Christ and the disciples—they take it for bible lore w/a grain of salt; but some of us actually believe these witness accounts. Some of us are sitting here in these mahogany pews scratching our heads wondering: *why doesn't it happen here? Why do we pray and immediately there are no results—as in the disciple's works 2,000 years ago?*

We have prayed en masse, and over a long period of time, some people are indeed reporting miracles. Loved ones cured, the disease not returning. Life sustained.

Maybe these are the slower-moving miracles, more difficult to see, less spectacular.

Don't run from My people in need when they come stumbling over to you.

Saw a handsome gay man. Red introduced himself. He felt very short.

Stood by a blax sistah, she smelled like mothballs. Wearing her best to Sunday service.

He reached deeper into the church with his eyes; and remembered his fantasizes of being so great in the eyes of God and so high in the sight of humanity.

Now he was getting a deeper meaning—which was simpler.

Go to church— for food, blessings, the most elemental of reasons.

His eyes traveled up the height of the cathedral, down to the mathematically spaced handsome dark mahogany burnished pews, empty of people.

I've began to see the love I've had certainly is not of a Christ-like style, but wider human style.

Life @ the bottom of the world. Upon hearing the guest preachers sermon he suddenly knew what the Lord(ess) had portended that AM. She spoke:

> We are living in one the richest most prosperous cities on earth. San Francisco is in the top 7% of the world's wealth. The outfit I wore last Saturday night could have fed 2 children in a developing nation for a decade.

She spoke about not being bought-out by the lure of money. There are forces that would give you money and beautiful things—which are not so beautiful when you look underneath.

PM
A big fat flyen' fucken' friggen' mess in hell. China VS. North Korea. The warlike nation of North Korea has been ruled by maniacs decades now—spending billions on war machines, while starving their citizens to skeletons. Their population is dying of near-starvation opportune disease.

Oh God this spellcheck is so conservative it makes me sick! *Genitalia*—says its wrong--but when finally get it right, it doesn't say so, just proceeds on to the next word…

There's a price for those fancy shoes.

Monday, February 18
Smile came to the OM's face as he thought of rent boys, hobbling down the street & others, passing saw; these others, younger, smiled for him.

& now the young lambs frolicking in the sun; & now the young lambs putting on the cloak & collar of Our Savior & now the young lambs entering into the convolutions which is Grace*

*--Which is all institutions of humanity; its so for the whole fucked up mess.

18

Coyote is packed w/people inside now, outside is no one, *vas est das?*
Many young—they are usually @ work—proving on this stray
holiday they have nothing else to do wit themselves. A lot of meals
go by me---eggs w/trimmings, toast, ham, green parsley garnishing; &
I'm wondering when they retire what will they too, do w/their spare
time?

I have said this before—wherever God places me higher or low—I'll
take it. In last Sunday's bible class we discussed the 3 sins Satan
offered our Savior. One—when he told Christ if you are hungry
change these stones into a loaf of bread—Christ's answer: *humans
will not live by bread alone.* The second was when said could,
command these stones to become bread, and Jesus said: *it is written
humans shall not live by bread alone*; and the third the devil took him
up to the highest turret on the temple and told him to jump off—
because ten thousand angels have charge of him— but Christ said: *it
is written you will not tempt the Lord your God.*

High hysterical but very loud volume voice fills the entrance of the
café; 2-pointed-toe knee-high boots appear in doorway. —The Bad
One is here---the OM was tired, his condition was that of coming
down from a sugar high—Thai fried bananas, & Thai ice coffee (2 of
them) on Sunday night w/Annie. Also Lemon Chicken—which is
sweet. He vowed not to order sweets from the Chinese restaurant
again—as he had already sworn off the Tomato Beef years ago.

His shoulder ached, still from *carrying* his books, pack (DIRTY
PICTURES, and POETRY Vol. 1, 2,) back/forth from The Infernal One for
2 days.

An artist doesn't have time for lengthy romance---one must sit,
pondering, brooding. Some of us get drunk. We must work
feverishly, tirelessly, to capture beauty, to capture thought, to capture
strength—on canvas, in manuscripts, in dance & architecture.

And the thirsty flock looked and saw on top of the hill --that much
spoken of place, a better place, that flowed with milk, honey, and all
good things; & no unpleasant, dangerous beasts there; a place of
peace & a place of plenty. After the long dusty march, a march of
hell, they had arrived in glory!

A crackhead has found a basketball hoop, looped his arm thru it, on his shoulder; jitters down the street. Will be lucky to sell it for $5, even $8. Maybe in desperation let it go for $2.

Searching for cigarette, pills; his demise will be sooner then most— maybe some people really cannot live in this world without aid. Jesus is not good enough for them, not even love from humans; nothing is good enough for them. They must anesthetize themselves against the horrors of earth, which are soon to come.

Maybe he can go to a place like Canada, Europe, & be maintained on his drugs. There is no criminalization of narcotics addicts there—for it is recognized as a mental health issue.

This is a greedy nation w/a great drive to provide illegal drugs in a trillion dollar commerce.

They will never allow legalization of drugs.

> Drugs make you feel absolutely nothing.
> --Teva; barriesta

Human hearts; wondering, longing.

Well—God sits up on High, faithful to this earth; S/He is the great timekeeper & S/He is The Eternal.

There is a reason, purpose, & a cause for me. Child Trans Boy in my playroom w/my microscope; there is a reason, purpose, a cause, for me to exist.

In front of Coyote FUCK SF POLICE scrawled on wall of parklett— graffiti —illegal by City standards; & this toxic ink must be cleared up by the owner—or his coffee shop will be slapped w/cash penalties.

PM
Nada

Tuesday, February 19

One thing about this town, better off people leave food, good food around in clean sacks cleanly on top of newspaper racks and ledges.

Think of Joe, who likes Punk style, sitting in jail w/no black fingernail polish.

Called to sign-in, read @ Easter Vigil.

The OM mumbled & grumbled down the street: *I'm so goddamn poor*—yet was it not he who had taken the vow of semi-poverty?

Wow, really cold weather here in SF, one of the coldest in memory.

Ahhh Gaggga! Owner's expensive ceramic pot thrown over into the street, broken! Puking thick black soil and flowers onto the asphalt! Vandals!

OM sat window seat with his free bread; he had spied ½ bag of Hawaiian potato chips in the café clean-up trey and nibbled @ those too. Again he'd had very little to eat that morning—leftovers.

Cool jazz toots.

Bright pink purple lavender hair, no teeth, crackhead dances in the street outside, falls down and gets up and dances some more, very thin. Busy gyrating—needs no food. Only crack.

T spied the Owner again fighting an ever-going battle w/forces of destruction—industriously scrubbing out the graffiti w/a toxic solvent-soaked rag.

A long time ago—we moved across the face of Africa in tribes— some tribe had no one to be their leader, they rapidly died out. A tribe led astray. OM, an Old Man, lived, knew and served his community w/the best advice he could.

A lot of the people keep walking—homeless or SRO dwellers— back/forth; up the Strassa & down. They do not stop—for they have not the barest coins, even for a cuppa.

Saw blax man walk by outside I-pod in hand; paused looking in the window of the coffee shop. T thought he was @ first a black business man, an entrepreneur—

Black man came in—made me uneasy—tho he was soft-spoken. Cool—wasn't sure why—observed later he is far older then first adjudged—lined face, grey, neatly trimmed natural; but now I see. He a playa'. When I went to the door just to look out into the fresh air of the street, a very sorry hooker, her pasty white face etched by time, was coming in quick, she walks way too fast, crookedly, w/the methamphetamine jitters. Weary T walked back inside—he had left his pack unguarded. Then he sees her perched right up next to the blax man—her pimp manager—T rushed back to his spot just in time to hear her say in High Agitation: *oh I left my crank back @ the house!*

So, she *is* a flying A-head, (not a crack hag) …

The pimp made several phone calls to the women he manages, crooning in mellow voice: *hi princess*, he outlined his plan for each of them that day—*how was your day today?* He made some arrangements on one woman's behalf for Internet/cable TV plan.

Sho' nuff is a black entrepreneur—he runs women, and most likely drugs.

That man is a snake w/a smile on his face.

Oh in addition to the other insults of the day—someone came in and stuck their hand in the tip jar & stole a $20 bill. The bariesta was all by himself that shift & he was in kitchen in back.

The sky darkens; age 16, 17, in New York, Greenwich Village every day a social feast—out on the streets, 100rds of gay kids; --back in Chi-Town, alone; blues every day; working all morning, afternoon, evening; hang out w/straight artists in club a few hours at night. Feast or famine.

There goes the older ultimate fabu-dressed panhandler woman— descending downhill to her small SRO hotel room crammed w/very expensive outfits of clothes—does she wonder—looking thru her outfits, assembling an ensemble for tomorrows work—she hustles 7 days per week, round the clock—does she wonder pensive, between folded sweaters, and power suits hanging in plastic bags: *how long can I keep on this routine?* How long will her legs hold out? Her ability to extend her hand to strangers for the extra coins she needs to keep her room—still rents go up.

Jesus Christ has told us it is the state of the heart; why do we forget the heart? —Gaunt old ugly men, women, walk past, unspoken too, feared, ignored. And very rich movie stars constantly re-arrange their faces to continue to appear beautiful—no wonder we ordinary people look so bad.

PM
Evidently there was a murder in South Korea high-rise apartment building—because of noisy neighbors. Now the big discussion TV news is that if they had known each other as friendlier neighbors this certainly would not have happened. How some Seoul high-rise apartments are setting up group activities for all their tenants; sharing monthly group meals. Good idea.

Wednesday, February 20, 11AM
Could not get back to sleep because of mild stomping above on ceiling. Must add that am on serious diet again—which may be part of it—had to eat all yesterday:

> A found bread
> Half bag salty BBQ potato chips (found)
> Coffee w/cream
> 1-pound ground beef
>   (small ketchup, Indian curry sauce)
> 3 large russet potatoes
> Raw greens juiced in water

And that was all! See if lost weight today. Try to repeat the same thing tonight. Going to Dean Jane Shaw's lecture—there will be food. But am allowed some variance. —It is what comes home to my house, which is all-important.

How could you be so stupid! This OM living in loneliness, poverty, ostracism, lack of dental care—who is busily grinding out 100 books—and you ignored that? Ha! Oh Foolish World Movers & Shakers!

Am hungry. Have nothing here in the house.

Finished editing I AM A SOUL--#2, must find a place to send it* very soon, so as to send the order to Text POD.
*---To Internet

The OM was now sleeping in 2 sweatshirts, a teeshirt, a hoody, and thin pajama bottoms. When he got uncovered from his blankie @ night, usually his feet & legs remained covered & his back, exposed, was warm enough to keep him from catching a cold.

PS everybody has been getting colds everywhere I go for the last 2 months. They fight it and fight it and then have to go to the doctors, or they take weeks but fight it off like I did. It's going around everywhere.

Bijou, white, taking a bath. —Takes 3 baths a year. Fluffed up, tail spread, water all over my floor outside her cage, dips beak into her drinking water cup fierce expression on face. Green Ariel bathes once per week. One from a desert breed, which seldom has sufficient rainwater to bathe in. Living in mountainous crags of sandstone rock.

Very very very dapper blax man on corner super clean, perfectly fitted tan slacks which zoom up pipe stem legs, matching vest; bowtie deep crimson red; same red in the designer bag he carries—very continental leather Italian shoes. He be clean tall sissy? Casually holds between 2 effete fingers the expensive shopping bag from ultra chic boutique; hails a cab—its horrible to think he might spend some time out here on this corner and not be picked up—compared to other races/shades; worse even to think he might be a criminal, disguised, and be picked up just to pull out a small handgun from his elegant coat and rob the cabby.

The OM scurries, he ran! He stamped his cane upon it! Green swirled in the air; $1 bill! He had been awaken by Hashem that AM and unable to get back to sleep—thinking then it might be a sign—of some kind; he'd really love to play the lotto now!

Saw first woman in front of the mosque today! Literally! The first Arabic, Muslim female standing in front of her place of worship! Have never seen a woman there before! –Not in my 11-years in this neighborhood. Always hoards, hoards, hoards, of men.

Oh my gawd, another tour bus! Transport for flocks of rich dot commies.

New wood frames rise to 3rd story; condos for the rich; the well-heeled.

Shrink

Sat on bus. The OM measured the color of the back of his hands to the hands of 2 white folks who sat on either side of him—white.

The blax bus driver had not lowered the stairs for him & he was pissed. Racist?

Outside the window, while they stopped @ a red light, he saw two transgender men-women pass by in the pedestrian zone as the bus rumbles in place:

> Bus driver: You see! (Jabs, finger pointing.)
>
> Blax Lady passenger: (Turns her head) Uhhh…
>
> Bus driver: Look @ that over there in the red.
>
> Lady passenger: I see; huh, uhhhhhh.
>
> Bus driver: Ain't that a shame.
>
> Lady passenger: That makes me mad!
>
> Bus driver: Uh uh uh.

25

Lady passenger: A lot like that... on the *low*... the down low. Uh huh, they ain't macho like we are.

The blax passenger lady didn't have her terminology right. It was all a crazy joke—right here in SF, capital of progressive-thinking. Hate; it was all a whirl...

Hell! --Youthful man shrieks out the window.

Ferry Building... *Campanili.*

Hole—Crazy Horse Gentlemen's Club; blond lays down legs spread legs in high heels.

Well you don't know the real thing—or the false—the young people outside w/clipboards gathering signatures to save the Sierra from being leveled... are they sincere, dedicated, doing a life-passion, or for money & don't care what their petitions says?

> I am barely earning a living @ this job. My rent is $700. It's an SRO. & we have to eat in the soup kitchen. I sighed up because I like the Sierra.

Transman sat in another window seat in the sun, in a different café — downtown—preparing to walk up the great hill to Grace—Dean Jane, & food.

All the abrasive things I've said about Grace, all the minor irritations & complaints, must remember it is true, of all priests all except one that doesn't exist! Ho ha ho ha! Whoops... well, *yes, Jesus does exist*... just not in this painful flesh, this foolish flesh like us!

A cathedral is usually the most splendid of all the churches in the dioceses. In cathedral—is the Bishop's Seat. The only one in the land.

Dr. Jane taught us that the first 3 centuries Christians were very persecuted—so the meeting place was not large—hidden. The early church was more face to face; people meeting in houses—it had to be proven: *yes we are really feeding the poor, teaching the Spirit; getting*

26

baptized; and accepting the stranger among us. It was a house-church.

Kry—Christ.

It has been the custom for millennium, when one power supersedes another, for them to build their temples, their palaces; their worship sites on top of the existing ones—usually on a grander scale. Often employing some of the materials from the conquered edifice, for their own. There are many reasons for this. One is usually that site is already pre-determined centuries before to be the best place—the highest, the most visible. 2nd often the bases of the old temple can be used for an additional reinforcement for the new temple. Wise minds decided that the site, thru the previous use of worship by the former rulers, must have— thru use— become already imbued w/special powers.

Colonnaded temples were built on pagan sites; hence the local people often confused the old religion & the new.

Haggi Sophia—holy wisdom.

A place to exhibit imperial power.

Theo takas; God barer.

Little people & their thrones!

Dedicated educators, study & prayer Orders. Thus one purpose— imparting spiritual information— for the new monasteries & nunneries springing up across Europe.

Bishops went to the feast & had a coterie of poor people with them— *look how I'm helping the community!*

The cycle of continuous prayer is important. & study. The monks & nuns copy manuscripts in their libraries, the calendar—the monistic orders were a haven for learning among the darkened lights of the Dark Ages.

Jolly well! Exclaims the Dean—she is from England too.

Get right down to the real nitty gritty.

A homeless woman I pass daily claims she is in need of something. Can't understand what she saying; it's not down to earth.

Tried to talk to her to do this/that; how to aid her in her plight, but by some fluke everytime the anger came out of her mouth garbled so none could understand barely a word she said.

One day I hope to teach, to get compassion; very few young peoples understand the meaning of this, nor stop & pass the time w/you.

PM
Nada.

Saturday, February 23, 12-Midnight
Have not wrote, have been sick—very sick w/food poisoning. Or extreme gastritis/threw up all food Wednesday nite, and lay on sick & vomit bedclothes thru Thursday in oblivion—did not take blood pressure medicine as was afraid to put anything in my stomach. Jasmin drove over and brought me vitamin C tablets to put in water, and picked up Penny's cat medicine from the vet & paid for it w/her pet care card.

Friday has just gone by and still sick but not the acute horrors of the constant throwing up unstoppable of Wednesday night pain in stomach. Was afraid could not go out to get food—but while speaking on the phone the Lord indicated to me my familiar clothes hanging on rack and showed me I could go out—and went across street to burrito shop and charged a beef burrito—no salsa. It is mostly rice, which is the recommendation for gastritis.

Jasmin suppose to come over tomorrow w/more supplies.

All the feelings—isolation, pain, desperation for the future of a crippled old senior.

Pain in gut.

Teetering around; changed bed sheets.

Bro Leo called several times. Dalora is suppose to deliver me more supplies tomorrow.

Saturday, February 23, 2PM
Dalora brought over supplies:

> Broiled chicken
> Boiled potatoes in tinfoil
> tunafish
> Toilet paper
> Paper towels
> Bleach
> Holistic cleanser
> Cat food — multi-flavors

Dean of a church—how much love do they give? They don't give love, their job is to manage the church. The priest of the church, how much love do they give? It is not their job to give love, their job is to perform the ceremonies. The congregants of the church—how much love do they give? They don't give love, they are too busy trying to hear the Word and figure out what God wants from them…

PM
Well I must say about these books & this life, I am dragging myself over battlefield of broken glass and sharp steel edges—by my bloody fingertips—that's how rough it is.

Have vowed—this Lenten season—to remove myself from the world one day ever week to sit home & rest. Relax. I can write. Go out just on one simple errand. That's it. Sleep very late, do not go rushing madly out of the house. One day of rest. Forget that being Sunday— God's day, because am busy @ church. So one day of rest it is!

> Thus says the Lord God, the holy One of Israel;
> In returning and rest you shall be saved;
> In quietness and confidence shall be your strength.
> Therefore the Lord waits to be gracious to you;
> Therefore he will rise up to show mercy to you.

29

For the lord is a God of justice; blessed are all those who wait for the Lord.
--Isaiah 30 15-18

Oh did I tell you--@ Wednesday class we discussed the evolution of Cathedrals from right after Jesus' resurrection to the present day.

For years of him being an atheist—he would hear songs containing religious lines, or see a movie w/religious statement and it would rattle his atheistic world. *Turn Turn Turn;* also *Amazing Grace;* such beauty in them—*didn't want to think they at all pertained to this God stuff*—which he equated to hypocrisy.

Sunday, February 24, 2PM
I guess the time is right to work for God after you have given up faith with the world—and it w/you; when you are a thing abandon.

This world is so hard because it is in inertia.

You must push & pull. Nothing comes easily. Everything must be moved by hand not by mind as in the higher realms.

It is the higher realms, which we see them, are so powerful so magnificent, but we can't get there just yet.

There are old songs came out whose lyrics seem to have higher social implications—most refer to human romance, but others can be about life, the meaning of existence, religion—*How Long Has This Been Going On?* Often think of the injustice of the earth suddenly uncovered. –To human's eyes as they have already been known to God.

Up hill towards church.

Saw senior white man; husky chap, is wet around his balls nested in his crotch; he had pissed on himself—which elders can sometimes do.

Easily walked up the hill! Am 8 pounds lighter!

I was on God's trail like a bloodhound, studying Latin, Greek, Hebrew.

30

Bible class.*

*Say here in the 19th of the Journal series that these 4:30 classes have been attending the last several years are not actually bible studies. In my haste to label them, and designate them apart from the centermost 6 pm worship service I tacked on the name *bible study*. The true bible study first been attending 7 years ago(?) Nearer to my beginning years w/Grace Cathedral—they were led by fine man Cannon Lampen, 95 years of age, and met 10am Thursday mornings. As tradition, we read thru the entire bible several scripture passages per session, and completed the whole bible in around a year? These 4:30 classes are scriptural based, but they are not bible studies. They are more ecumenical studies.

In class we discuss this interesting book The Sound Is Our Wound or something like that; in which repeated a fact, today's modern birds have an urban bird song measurably changed in resonance to the rise of human noise! The birds are singing louder to be heard over us!

More people are gathered together in mega cities then ever before in humanity.

The noise of the sound of lament.

Lamentations was probably written around 500BCE or later; after destruction of the first temple and its community committed to exile; the Jews carried off to be slaves.

We are all exiles we live in a state of exile, this is why we lament; not a question of if but *how*.

We spoke of so many who had left their families to come to SF— because of gender discrimination in their home states—and others disaffected by emotional, mental problems; those without families, those with broken childhoods who also come to SF—then someone suggested that some extremely intelligent people left their communities because they are incredibly bright, come here & gather together and get $200,000 a year jobs, displacing the poor.

One parishioner stated the following:

I went to airport which was completely quiet when I landed @ 4AM & decided to rest—but the airport has giant TV's blaring and garbage cans w/automatic trash compactors. — Any garbage dropped into it activates the trash compactors. Whenever someone threw a cup in it the whole machine begins to roar and bang to compact the cup. –For just one tiny cup.

Spiritual sense is born to the suffering. We are born carnal, hedonistic. It is only thru suffering that we are reborn. That we attain the spiritual.

Martin Luther King said that we walk along a horizontal road, at one point we will encounter a wall, —the only way to go is to ascend.

During the service it was indicated to look at the Greek letter symbol for Christ, gold on the marble floor and from there up to the ceiling-- a lofty 7 stories above them he saw a brightness, of Jesus standing right there, right next to him on his right hand side.

They were giving Oscar away on TV glitz when he and Annie descended the hill to the burrito shop—waiting for T's laundry. Beef burrito for me. The young Chinee ordered 4 plates of avocado and mushrooms, —claiming that was all she had to eat that day. A small fortune! As a single dish is costing $7!

Puts us in touch w/death the possibility of dying—especially @ my age, I am not happy. This is how I feel tonight.

The un-comfortability of living w/death.

PM
Well further this scripture says: *in returning and rest will be our strength—yet we would not. We say no, we will flee upon horses, and ride upon the swift.* Isaiah 30 15-21

South Korea new lady president states in her address speech North Korea should stop posturing nuclear war and depriving its citizens to starvation and turning its back on the entire international community. Serious talk—while on stupid American TV—the Oscars! Urhgugh! Frills! Glitz! Superficiality!

Monday, February 25
Am in Coyote first time in a week—got small coffee, my latest idea—
50¢ cheaper.

A piano concerto fills the air.

Outside the plate glass window, a fallen TV girl sashays past—nearly
naked; bare long brown arms, legs, torso; an ostrich feather is her
primary costume; dipping on bony knees in ill-fitting women's
pumps; alongside her, a male companion walks, his air of resignation
to her spectacle; air of: *oh well, what can I do about it? This is her!*
She has stringy thin bikini g-string thong w/tassels sewn on a belt
over & bra; very skinny & no tits. Dips of her bony knees; gangling
walk.

In the background, @ entrance a piteous whine—followed by sharp
admonition: *LOLA!* ---Hawk has made his entrance w/a hysterical
voice.

The music changes… is it… no… could it be? Can you believe? Just
as Hawk sits down @ table, the owner puts the Funeral Dirge on the
sound system! The Funeral Dirge from— Chopin; (Piano Sonata #2
Funeral March).

Could we change it from the Death March? Cries a plaintive voice of
a female customer…

Thick pianist's hands striking cords.

Hit with high note, grand finale.

Reminds me of a past time of drawing rooms in palatial castles, grand
parties on invitation of the rich.

Inevitable, whims of the rich can elevate, or crush a multitude of poor
people dependant on them.

There is all kinds of beginnings people have. Some come from a very
good home, safe, so happy they don't even realize they are poor.

I got to work, work, every daaaay!
--Pop Song

The rich don't live in a world like we the workers. Not @ all.

I got my last silver dollar. They got a million more silver dollars.

PM
My jaw nearly dropped off! TV, progressive European station does a special on the Bosperous district of Turkey, which is being gentrified and the poor driven out—the rich moving in—but there are 800,000 luxury apartments sitting empty—they can't find enough rich to buy them.

Roma are driven out, and other groups. All poor. The words of these people mimicked what I've been saying in my Journal for years!

Tuesday, February 26

Pretty cool show.

I wish I had my buyers there.

Black suitcoats, ties, polished shoes, satchels; the rich salesmen of the dot.com era; talk of buying & selling in the tens of thousands of dollars. One beside them, ancient, Asian, so thin, back bent, caries a load of glass bottles, aluminum cans, for recycle --for pennies.

The path has been indicated to me—*you see how I have stumbled. Jesus.* The path. Hides in a black comforting cloud—we must do the work, which in our soul we may choose & we can't be forced.

Preparing to go to Grace; prepare food for tomorrows serving in SRO hotel run by Episcopal Services.

Chopped hot dogs, helped miscellany, stood working 1.5 hours—then dined well!

PM

(Dr.) Helena's next patient is schizophrenic & lives alone.
--Documentary about Cuba by woman filmmaker.

This is sad to me, that to have a mental illness relegates one to lifelong loneliness.

Cuba spends over 10% of its annual budget on education. The USA, only 2%.

12-students per class. America, 20, or more.

Wednesday, February 27
The constriction rises 6, no, 7 stories. Condos for the rich.

Drama in the sky! 2 small birds—parrots (?) —race, screeching across the air high up. Lower level a small flock of 8 pigeons flies for cover to top of 5th story building—then off of it to the roof of another down the street.

There it is. Predator! A falcon of some kind! Large thick wings flap steadily, powerfully, oaring its way thru air like a massive boat. Strong, gliding across the scene looking for pray. 2-seagulls circle.

Grace. The Operative is very nice; says to bring in my new rent receipts! May be going to give me additional monies!

Tall white European woman very well dressed tasteful clothes, very expensive knee-high boots, opens door to expensive bistro for her party:

> She has a trust fund.
> --Overheard

Last nite @ Grace preparing dinner for their SRO— took us 1 hour and a half to prep the food---to chop chop chop vegetables, and the hotdogs. Just 20 minutes to eat. All what I've been doing these last 40 years is the prep work!

Wind blew harsh up the hill; the lecture is to start in 25 minutes.

The marble floor around the bema was so ultra polished it looked like water—as a moat, a lake of water surrounding the alter.

900 AD formation of monasteries comes to Europe. Reclamation of these already fallen monasteries w/reforms a short time later.

Cathedral is a seat of power both government & religious as well as for our common worship.

The monastic, the clergy, created an educated class. Set up centers of learning in their churches; they are powerful & have a huge reach— reach out to other monastic centers across Europe & beyond.

Romanesque are the rounder more sturdy cathedrals; gothic is sharp, soaring.

Sites chosen are next to rivers, on top of hills.

Cathedrals like fortresses, built on a hill.

Long nave; transepts on either side. The middle, where the horizontal & vertical cross, is the heart of the Cross. Where is situated the alter table.

Rule of church teaching to the people who are constantly thinking: *where are we going after this life?*

The poor in those days—the vast majority of people—were hungry most of the year. Life was short. They lived in 1 room houses w/no windows, and slept w/a horse or cow inside. The 100 years war was going on, men were dying, coming home w/injuries. Of course their main question was: *what is going to happen to me next after I die?*

Cathedral designed to have the congregants constantly lifting their eyes upward.

Tracery, are the lead pieces between glass in the stained glass windows; that holds them in place.

These mighty cathedrals inspire a great sense of the miraculous—by their architecture.

> The first time I came to Grace Cathedral I wondered why nobody told me I was going to hell, that I was wrong—like they do in Hong Kong—.
> --Annie, Chinese

PM

Japan was an imperial power during the late 1930's, to mid 40's, they invaded other Asian nations, including the sovereignty of China, and set up brothels for their Japanese soldiers, making forced-prostitutes of Chinese, Taiwanese, Korean, women; including a few white women who fell into their hands, from the Netherlands, captured during war. These women were called Comfort Women.

Japan has still not admitted her wrongdoing in this shameful and barbaric practice over 70 years ago. 150 Comfort Women have been located in China and elsewhere and put in a book written by a Chinese scholar, Su Zlaing, is his name.

Most Comfort Women brothels were instituted in China. 100rds of thousands of women.

Before the girls were sent into China they were forced to have their uteruses removed before they were shipped to the brothels.

Forced sterilization to prevent pregnancy—most inconvenient for a woman forced to be prostitute.

Instituted by Japanese military girls 16-years old captured & forced into captivity. Servicing 5 or 6 men in a row. This forced prostitution was enforced by military power and national forces who created this situation—so it constitutes war crimes.

Up to this day Japanese deny the fact. Tho it was implemented by the Imperial Japanese.

This shows diabolic level of planning, foresight, intent, to debase another human being for their convenience @ utmost efficiency. A great sin.

37

150 comfort women have been located in China. 234 in Korea.

Many have died, most cannot come forward to speak of their ordeal—the actual number of them, it is calculated into the thousands of women.

Thursday, February 28, 12-Noon Dentist Day
Just saw David Young V got job as building manager, block from the old torture chamber of his former employment. *Its all I can do* he said.

I told him: *You don't need a big fancy job <u>thinking</u>—It's bad for art to take any job too serious. You can't take a job home w/you. I worked for years @ shit jobs. Ones where you don't think—and keep your mind free for art!*

Subway; a tribe of kindergarten children squeal, clustered like a passel of geese.

A short black sissyman, attired elegant—sighs like a buxom diva chanteuse. I walk.

Mission District.

The old Victoria theatre—former deluxe striptease theater now for rent. She is battered, and set in a raunchy neighborhood; newspaper, waste paper blows across her frontage which must be swept away daily, and homeless encamp in her entrance underneath the marquee—yet she prevails.

The old Stage Door is open… inside a glimpse of brand new costumes clean, pressed, frilly; all colors; a push broom, a new dolly carrying truck; her tall wings have sets draped w/veils; the scenes wait to be lifted into place; a pink telephone…

A robust, musical, young man asks if he can help me; informs me: *it's a musical, going up tonight!*

Here I am for my apt. Native American Dental clinic--what! *You are filed under the wrong list—homeless. Program not eligible—so we have to charge you a lot more then before.*

I feel week & drained; think I must still be sick.

It's always something—bad. It wears you down. *Well I'm almost 70 years old don't that count for anything?* I says.

Day goes down; swaths of light; brilliant; orange w/heart of sunset @ the edge of the world; black mountain, fuzz of trees; soon the sun sets behind them, the world goes dark.

PM
Nada

Friday, March 1, 1PM
Tired of fighting all this inertia. 68-years of it.

Young people dressed in pink w/pink face paint like hi-tek native red people, run up/down in the downtown streets—18-24 year olds all consulting their electronic I-pods; the kids are playing some kind of mass game; *students;* this is essentially a college campus this is what its like to live on a campus?

Are we looking for a church? They yell excitedly.

Block down, here are some more, but these kids are green & blue. They run back/forth across the street taking pix of themselves on cameras & cellphones. Up-scale older young people cast a wary eye on these kids from inside coffee shops & boutiques.

The further up the blocks you go the less trouble there is for polite humans. Go on up from O'Ferrell to Geary—Geary will be less problematic. Both these streets are the current definition of the outside edge of the TL, a very rough area indeed.

I think it is a mistake to say we are the same—FTM & MTF—we are not. We have different sets of survival issues, different life-goals. Perhaps we even differ in what transpires in the womb that cause us to

39

be trans-formed by a set of reasons also; science does not know; we are different and probably should have separate facilities for different needs, unless, like the idea that we should come together in unity as trans brothers & trans sisters; it is a noble one, but it usually does prove difficult, it doesn't work! We tolerate one another at best.

Many people who have lived The Life are going to recount deeds they did whither horrific or mild.

Anxiety was part of his diagnosis so nervous today—there was a problem w/the blood panel, it had detected something wrong and now the Japanese doctor was telling him, that his Hep C was on the chart.

He did not know to what quantity this was—he needed a second test for that, so one was scheduled, immediately next week.

In Laundromat watching laundry dry. Blue throw-up blankets & PJ's revolve round & round.

PM
Some people are capable of great acts of kindness & love, but can't sustain it, being a basically mean people. They have been made mean by circumstance.

Saturday, March 2
You're worth it—said the Lord—he had earned his lunch.

Some notes taken about today-- working backwards from the latest to the first:

Encountered Nicole, The Hen, on street beside Mayflower:

> Joi Cook is dead. She died on the night of the Oscars. She was a poet. She always liked you. She called you, *'Red, my cheese-eating friend.'*

> Joi died of liver cancer. She used drugs to modify her mental illness, and later alcohol. She had quit drinking but then went back to drinking and her liver gave out. She was bi polar but could not take her psyche meds because of her bad liver.

40

Some people have so much hell put on them.

So many conditions.

So much pain on earth.

Which sends pangs to my heart, chiefly about what will become of me? And, where will my work go? Nowhere popular, but straight into historical archives, into some soon-forgotten moat; categorized such as: *unimportant irregular prints.*

Before that, sat in Quetzal and spoke with Cosmo. He has still another new boy toy, who he met as a friend of the old toy who has broken himself on drugs—crank—and is a broken Ken Barbie doll— off crank. Joe being one of the earlier broke boy toys—broke off Heroin. Cosmo told me, says: *oh, Joe got your money but hates to write people. He is engaged in prison in self-betterment classes, and weight lifting.* My prayer for him is still going on.

Cosmo has lovely green eyes. We spoke of many & sundry things.

Before that spoke to brother Will— ex-Grace Priest, who now has his own parish. Before that Brother Leo and another soul bro he met online who wanted pointers on transition. We spoke of trans stuff, ideas; I gave them some suggestions, and wish well for the brother. Also, Leo is soon to receive another surgery, but have to push it thru the medical plan first. All this is what we trans go thru—pushing forward our medical plans, in a way, which is trans, gender, specific—and would not be necessary for an illness like a broken foot or high blood pressure.

Back to Priest Will. We spoke together of a greater vision of a greater ministry—both of us not knowing what we are speaking of—but that it is itching in our souls and a great longing—spiritual longing— is filling our sails, so I at least, and I believe bro Will too are ready to hop in the boat and set sail the minute the Lord(ess) blows that gust to fill our hearts—in fact we are both already in our individual boats right now, waiting on God!

Here is just the barest jist of what we said:

41

Red: I feel I'm marking time in the church I'm learning, but how am I going to apply this learning to my work, and what exactly is my work and its something about going out into the world with this work—which I don't know what it is. I think the church is wonderful, but it isn't going far enough. It takes us right up to the edge of reality, then stops with us still looking out of the windows, but not moving anywhere!

Priest W: Revolution is the word.

Priest W: A change within, and without. Not a revolution that tears down or destroys, but a change within, and without, and somehow the two meeting.

PM
People who work as prostitutes often form over-inflated sense of value of themselves--for the wrong reasons.

Sunday, March 3
He walked onward towards shul—church—somewhat woozy. Am not had enough to eat & replete w/fattening hot dogs am waiting to get food cards & money--after 5oclock the food stamps will be activated. Slightly pissed having gained back 2 pounds of the precious 8 shed during my mal-ease urgh.

Whoo, ZZZ cars, I have seen the bad traffic rules they break in haste which is damaging inevitably to the pedestrians.

Came in Cathedral in midst of lovely organ recital.

Trills! Sonorous booms!

We are reminded of Christ, to be eternally grateful to God.

The organist takes a bow—

Oldest parishioners engaged in the eternal running of Christ's business, Denis stops by for a chat. Bearded, trim figure, bright blue eyes under his spectacles.

To do justice is even greater then supplication; –when you're bowing feverently to the Eternal—where are your sisters, mothers, & daughters who are left out of the mosque because they are female?

Same can be said to the orthodox Jews and any other orthodox sect.

Amazingly small religious study only 3 regulars in class & 2 visitors. Where is everybody? Is the fiscal cliff keeping them @ home worried?

Have I told you this mess in government if the two wings--republican & democratic of our administration's albatross don't flap together, once the deadline of March 1st is reached, 50-thousand teachers will be laid off. Many cuts to government and Social Services— meaning the cutting of government and civil service jobs. It is bad. It is drastic. Does it explain why I have made no sales this month? I'm sure my readers are from the beleaguered middle class…

T sat there in the mightily small group wondering where everybody was. He was worried. —What cuts was the government going to make? How might they apply to him?

The small study was not exactly what he needed for his soul or heart—simply ordinary chatter.

Out in the cold alone. No church. No nothing.

Meeting after church service many people say they aren't happy. Not w/all this new configurations. I have the horrid thought—the people in charge: *are they trying to kill this service?*

At the meeting no one spoke as vehemently angry as they had privately, so on the surface all seems well and is rolling along.

PM
My food cards were not there, disappointment. Did not meet up w/A., for she was not there. The service was not especially good—maybe the lack of enough meat/protein today and yesterday was the reason.

Not a special night at church—kind of low key, not sad but melancholy—and this is not God! I'll tell you!

It is hard to concentrate on worship when you have not had enough to eat—plain and simple.

Now back to grind out I AM A SOUL-3, to get to Bancroft. Rush.

Jesus fucken' H. Christ! Syria nation in flames, fighting despots, & roving rebels; Europe in turmoil. America falling over the financial cliff to the ruination of her poor and the destruction of her middle class—all this reported on German, French, English TV, and RT— Russian TV—but on our own domestic American TV—<u>Hollywood!</u> The Oscar award nite scandals!

We grasp @ God to dominate God, to twist God around to get what we desire.

Monday, March 4
25th floor. Took psyche meds out of my canister & put them in pocket. Fear of heights.

Sit here wait to take blood test. Worries:

> Liver test
> $30 short on rent
> Can't reach librarian @ archivist library

Finally, in office got a hold of Bonnie, and am squared away for this Friday. Whew!

Heard cylinders rolling around as elevator descends 25 floors.

The OM encountered that day the deranged woman who begs w/cat daily on the SF streets. Her horror story --is being evicted in 30 days. He said he'd send off some emails and try to get some results:

> I'm afraid of being in the streets. I'll get killed. Where can I go
> w/my cat? I'm afraid of the shelter, I'll get raped. I can't live like
> this.

44

He took her problems on, to small degree, emailing 2 pastors he knew. He was in the system, she is not. The woman is 61, just under the old-age level. A caseworker would know how to handle it so she could be housed—but she doesn't have a caseworker.

Walked down to pay Rent.

Thankfully his food stamps were in. He got a burrito on the stamps down in TL, and groceries.

But when the OM went to his mailbox a new horror he discovered. A hideous notification-- Summons from the Superior Court!

PM
Nada.

@ desk the Old Man leans back in his chair from hours of Journaling. He has dreams of justice.

Tuesday, March 5
@ first the Lord(ess) has been summoning me for small tasks—like crossing the street out of my way to give words of encouragement to a dying soul—whose flickering flame is extinguishing in the white winter of Amerikkka Kapitalist Pharaoh empire.

Spoke to cat lady—she tells me the latest hysterical details of her impending eviction, crazed—as anyone who has no place to live after this April 15, having been more or less housed for the last decade---if she's telling the truth.*
*--If she knows what the truth is.

Food cards not there! But Amazon paid out well! $40 the last day of February! By the sweat of my brow—I am saved! Thank God.

Annie (Chinee) out of kindness has driven me to Trader Ho's to PU supplies, & then to din!

If you live in a big city and you have 4 or 5 friends who are well off and they treat you say, once or twice a month to dinner or a show---so this amounts to several times a week you are getting treated between all of them, it brightens your life. You are surrounded by art, culture, a diversity of people—some of it free experience; but if you live in a desolate area, poor, no art galleries nor libraries, and people all of a very low education—and nothing free, life is bleak, it is harder to sustain day after day, year upon year, decade upon decade—finally there is only 3 or 4 escapes. To go mad. To find religion. To resort to drugs.

PM
In case haven't mentioned, am *counseling* a woman who regularly panhandles w/her cat on her horrendous renter eviction come April. She also produced a summons from the police for alleged prostitution—of a *female* decoy cop.

Told her:

> This is just harassment, because you are a regular panhandler, and they are trying to force you off the street.
>
> This is all I need I have so much to worry about already, I can't stand one more thing.

And Transman thought privately how he'd just thought the identical thing the night before upon receiving Summons from the Superior Court—not realizing it was for *Jury Duty*.

When I finished the last few pages of I AM A SOUL, I saw the passage about the mad man, and dealing w/bad spirits that inhabit a person. If one is to be a healer they must have some knowledge of this.

We are hiding. We do not know the true extent of ourselves. Our capabilities. God reveals this to us as we grow.

There are weighty issues to deal with.

Why would one want to command the evil spirits in a diseased person—for healing, out of compassion, out of love? Out of anger that such a thing is possible that an evil spirit would plague an *innocent* person?

What is your *motivation?* As the Hollywood movie directors say…

Turned to the bible for solace, and it opened @ chapt. 7 or thereabouts, Mathew—Jesus instruction as to not worry what you will eat, or what you will wear—just go out on the Journey; and Jesus is admonishing Her/His apostles & followers to go out into the world upon their healing, preaching, teaching ministry. After Transman finished I AM A SOUL, w/that passage, he sat relaxing in front of the TV (public education channel) and realized his spirit was vexed. Just as it had been when Jesus, 20' high, had come to him down the aisle of Grace Cathedral, just standing there waiting for some word from him—he was perplexed.

Yes I want this work, and I will do it! he said.

Here is that passage:

> Time has begun for me to begin! Beyond You there is no other. Those who work for the Eternal, and keep Her/His Commandments—are blessed.

> Grace Cathedral is the place T received his training before he starts on his ministry.

> An interesting occurrence happened. It was the Old Man's habit to march briskly along the streets carrying home his purchases, and stopping every few blocks to perch on a fire hydrant or building ledge—like a chair—to rest. On the final blocks a blax homeless man, extremely disheveled and speaking wildly to thin air stopped a few feet from the Transman and began to pace in circles mumbling in an awful way. T thought—*he is my brother, but there is nothing I know how to say to him. I can't handle this madness.* And was a bit worried if the man would begin some crazy rant @ him and drive him from his perch. He thought of Jesus commanding the evil spirits to come out of insane people 2000 years ago. And immediately @ this thought the man turned and walked off across the street.

> The Old Man pondered while he walked home: *the spirits can read human minds—whither they are good spirits or bad—they see more, they hear more. Even my bird can read some of my thoughts* (documented in Journals). *Maybe the evil spirit saw Jesus in my thoughts and beat a*

47

hasty retreat—least it too be driven from its comfortable foul and awful abode—a sick human soul.

A lot of this is *instruction*; it is not just Presto Change-O!

A lot of it is instruction.

Now here is a breakdown on the ranking of some vital gifts. I soon must provide you w/the hierocracy of gifs—for the ability to cast out demons is a gift:

A Reading From The First Letter Of Paul To The Corinthians:

> If I speak in the tongues of mortals and of angels, but do not have love, I am a noisy gong or a clanging cymbal. And if I have prophetic powers, and understand all mysteries and all knowledge, and if I have all faith, so as to remove mountains, but do not have love, I am nothing. If I give away all my possessions, and if I hand over my body to be burned, but do not have love, I gain nothing.
>
> Love is patient; love is kind; love is not envious or boastful or arrogant or rude. It does not insist on is own way; is not irritable or resentful; it does not rejoice in wrongdoing, but rejoices in the truth. It bares all things, believes all things, hopes all things, endures all things.
>
> Love never ends. As for prophecies, they will come to an end; as for tongues, they will cease; as for knowledge, it will come to an end. For we know only in part, and we prophesy only in part; but when the complete comes the partial will come to an end. When I was a child, I spoke like a child, I thought like a child, I reasoned like a child; when I became an adult, I put an end to childish things. For now we see in a mirror, dimly, but then we will see face to face. Now I know only in part; then I will know fully, even as I have been fully known. And now faith, hope, and love abide, these three; and the greatest of these is love.
> --1 Corinthians: 13-1-13.

There is a scripture, which actually ranks the spiritual gifts—the minute I find out what it is, you will see it appear in this journal!

48

I must say, I am adverse often, to seeing church people from my past, because I live now within my own comfortable theology--@ Grace; tuning out the Our Fathers, and stuff I dislike like an unpleasant static on a radio frequency, and learning, climbing up the ladder of spiritual awareness @ my own pace and God's pace for me. I don't like being around challenging liturgical arguments, or rehashing the gay-going-to hell stuff, or no women priests, or the heavily dominated patriarchal verbiage—am so far beyond that, that when someone recently known from 20 years ago made contact, I have put off returning the call—because just don't want to subjugate myself to that mess anymore! Some are comfortable w/it no doubt; I am not!

Wednesday, March 6,

Pray for all people. And these who form our church.

Especially the sheep.

> Sales Center Opening Spring 2013.
> 70 Condos.

Crow perched on billboard hunches its shoulders, bobs to push out a vehement **CAW!** Croaking & rasping from it's bird lungs.

A. says she fears the Dentist next week—*my emotional pain is bad enough, too busy to deal w/physical pain too!*

The sky was a great collision of grey swaths, & dark grey swaths plummeting diagonal across the sky like an artists painting wiped w/oil cloth.

Setting up Journal number 19—LIFE AT THE BOTTOM OF THE WORLD.

PM
Was by Coyote briefly today; saw some of the old guys.

It is quite obvious some of our old people are just waiting to die.

Thursday, March 7,

Something beautiful is rising! Dome shape, building to 6th floor height; dome; modern clean line architecture—but its not for us!

God(ess) sent us Karl Marx to explain this situation –to break it down for us.

Red rode trolley to his Dr.'s apt to see his liver panels. He heard in his mind the dreams of Hugo Chavez, Karl Marx, Fidel Castro— Transman Red saw the people of earth & animals.

The rich—what kind of people are they? Who can order servants around & command employees w/the wave of a hand; hail taxicabs with a upraised gesture & a pose; snap of fingers summon waitresses for standard tips.

They cheat, they bargain, dealing death, rob; but worse it is the poor among us, striving to become rich who will be our new masters.

Old Man had taken his vow of semi-poverty but he was always complaining about this poverty as if it was not a choice—angry & complaining about his condition that made him and people of this earth poor.

Vow of semi-poverty is as you know the next thing to the vow of poverty which nuns, priests, and some aesthetics take.

Came upon a small person in the clinic:

> I saw you @ a conference about 7 years ago, you so inspired me.
> Got up there and said how you'd beat the system.

T didn't hardly feel he'd beat the system, but was glad he had inspired her/him. This individual is an artist too & poor.

S/he said:

> Its so hard out here.

Its so cold out! Good thing he had his warm hat w/earflaps.

Older gay man sits in outdoor plaza where the Castro trolley turns around, on the intersection of Market St; does he recall his youth? Next table are 4 youthful gays. One makes a sign 4 fingers sliding up and down inside a slick hole…

The huge malevolent sandstone building towers over the city from out of its roots in Battery Park—landfill next to the grey/blue water of the bay. It is the Stank Of America building—it can be seen from every corner of the city, it towers so high. Its eyes are upon us. Eyes of kkkkapitalism on all of us.

Pop-up thoughts of small enterprise vs. korporate kapitalism.

Drugs are their comfort.

Well—I guess you put a prayer out & wait but it takes a long damn time…

For the soul-sick weary sleeper to respond to the prayer for him/her & slowly uncurl his fetal form of defense, the fist clench, into something trusting, receptive, able to change & grow.

Just encountered another young person—who working 2 jobs— barrista minimum wage. He at the acquisitional egregious Fucks (StarFucks) which does pay medical & this young man is in need of an operation—his country South of the Border does not provide. The Fucks hires all—especially noted for hiring us trannys—and pays beneficent health care. But everything else they do is the Fucks:

> There was a stopping place in the middle of town—everybody went there for coffee and small snacks. Then Fucks moved in across the street. They sold their coffee at half price. That is 75¢ for a $2. cup of coffee—and were prepared to do this as long as it takes. After a year, the whole town had switched sides and was buying cheap coffee. The original home-grown shop went out of business; the minute they were gone, the Fucks raised their prices back to normal. They had cornered the market.

The Old Man sat @ counter to listen to exciting music & watching the street roll past. He wondered how he'd pay to do his laundry… 8

more days till Grace bestowed him w/grant monies largess of those far better off then he.

Pigeon cozzied up on building cornice 5th story; the sky is theirs; black feather preen, ruffle, behind her grey/blue sky, clear, blocked by nothing.

There are no flowers now outside Coyote—they must lay dormant; it is more cold-weather plants, w/some little white flowers but their roots work the soil to prepare for the flowers of Spring—the lovely gay flowers.

Again man who is a woman goes by; beautiful skin & rounded behind and round shoulders indicate use of female hormone estrogen. —Her long beautiful hair is curled in a ball & pinned to her scalp in a quasi-male style. Her full lips; petulant. She walks in a slower undulating movement as some real women, & not fast-efficient clip of a he-she looking for men trade. One day now she will bloom forth in feminine abundance.

The drumbeats of social justice pounded feverishly in his mind; the OM swooped upon his infernal NOTES sheaf.

All; says the Lord. *All, all I said All. ALL!*

Fat & skinny. Poor and rich. Kkkkapitalists & dissolute. All genders, all types, all people in My soul where I have inhabited them; they are MINE!

T felt quite good. He'd received a compliment that day—from a thin young person without a lot of power.

You've been an inspiration to me.

Red Jordan Arobateau
Tuesday, March 25, 2013
4AM, Pacific Standard Time
San Francisco, CA

Part- 2

He thought: *will this new Pope make a difference? To the nuns? For the rise of women? —Will the Catholic Church reorganize itself?*

I will set My house right; says the Lord(ess).

The gigantic 20 floors high condos for the rich on Van Ness Ave., directly across from the new hospital to be built— blocked out the sun from the humble Coyote—2 blocks away.

Some are loving & kind, peaceful, & advantaged, but so confused it nullifies all the good they can do. Too bad.

PM
Junkies; slouching alcoholics; fighting; no peace.

The street where dreams are smashed.

Its hard. This world is so hard.

For all.

Even the green sea turtles. Who live 100-years. Bobbling in the ocean. Occasionally climbing onto land to lay their eggs & incubate them by the warmth of their bodies covering the nest mound.

> Gross National Happiness is our nation's greatest resource.
> --4th King of Bhutan

Friday, March 8,
Romanesque pillars, marble white; Congregational Church, no more —its a shell, purchased by the Arts College. Grecian columns; white, imposing entrance; stately. Prime realestate investment.

He would save cats and dogs.

On way under the tube—to Berkeley.

The long ride under the heavy million-ton water of the Bay. Prayed it never, never, springs a leak.

The train rushed towards the Bancroft. Towards funds. He didn't know what he'd do with the remainder of the day—maybe this would be enough.

Saw bright strong woman in West Oakland; blazing-eyed, dominant.

Subway station was full of screaming howling brats. OM thought—*among these dozens and dozens is a fraction—my future readers. A few of these will be led to discover me thru the stacks…*

Little animal w/golden tan paws runs out of forest of rustling dead leaves onto the asphalt walk, begs for food. —Beggars! All squirrels!

Homeless beg for coins; animals, for food!

He had realized after the years now all this excitement, carrying to the Bancroft—his soul-searching grunts entirely went to pay his rent!

Came out on SF side to fierce winds—cold. Flags on the banks flap wild.

Winds wild due to wind tunnel artificially created by 10-story buildings.

Staid suits in Coyote—talking about:

>   Flipping
>   Cash flow
>   1.5 million in trade
>   3.75 million out

That kind of crap & I'm in here @ the counter counting pennies for my next cuppa coffee.

Here are the graphs, your money back in five years… one suit says to another.

I guess God must put enough nut cases on earth—people who will never be all right—for the rest of us to caretake.

What does this mean? 130% of your money back!

Across the way @ the tavern across the street, the painter paints slowly, small human figures emerge on the wood panel; I see arms, I see legs...

That first 500 thousand dollars that comes in!

2 Caucasian bums covered/grime, engrained, so their skin has turned grey. Smoking crumpled butts of cigarettes.

A giant poodle w/liquid eyes strains its leash to see me. Animals close to the heart. Know more then we do—

More flesh-tone arms, legs, appear on the panel across the street.

Had a little rip-roarin' conversation w/across-the-hall neighbor:

3, 4th generation is ok. The first, 2nd, we have to worry about.

Yeah, because the first is training the 2nd. If *we* could train them they'd be alright.

Remember that Indian family flushing diapers down the toilet. The whole plumbing system backs up...

Then T mentioned the idiots from the Island who lived above him:

8 people in one tiny studio apartment, consisting of one room --but he has a good job and his wife works too. Selfish pigs. Greedy money-grabbers.

Somebody is dumping wet garbage in the recycling bin.

Yeah and the man in the basement takes it back out; carries upstairs to the first floor & sets it in the hall w/a nasty note.

An African-American sissy bourgiee man, so upscale he squeaked, talked w/us in the Laundromat, he said the gi-normous amount of rent he was paying ($1,500 for one small studio room). Talked to him and

57

it appeared the worst of it all wasn't the price, but the struggle when he'd go out to look @ a place there would be a hoard of 30 yups waiting for the same place: *so competitive, you go out to all these interviews; thought if I ever have to move again, to find a place---its credit check and income requirements…*

Young peoples ensemble: sneaker's, hoodies, back packs, skateboard.

PM
Well shiet! How about this!—

> By April 1906, his dictating was going full steam ahead, without a charted course. Like its predecessor, the volume mingles a diary-like record of Mark Twain's daily thoughts and doings with fragments and pungent portraits of his earlier life.
> --Benjamin Griffin Editor, Mark Twain Project, from Newsletter of the Friends of The Bancroft Library

This is exactly what I did in AUTUMN CHANGES (My Unofficial Semi-Autobiography) –mix!

@ slavery's end in America, there were 4-million slaves. A white man has written a very interesting book about it.

Young barrista in Coyote confided in me something, which I'd been thinking about recently myself: *I think everybody in SF is crazy.*

Saturday, March 9
Sun out. Summer is back!

There is a perfectly good man laying on the sidewalk has all his working parts; but he is crushed. An alcoholic, drug-user. He sleeps in the streets—w/bugs. He could be of very good use to society, to other people.

You prepare a table before me in the presence of my enemies—all 3 are @ my back—right behind me. The truth was before Transman when he saw again in his mind what the evil one he said to him. Miss Celeste has rejoined the group. Because she has nowhere else to go. He saw they were funning together—it was compelling—but God wanted him to associate w/people of a higher mind.

You will be invited, says Jesus—to a higher court.

I want you to go further—says the Lord. *Get more use*. (Out of me.)

Rev Will explained it to me—protestant and catholic. —The Protestants ask: *what can God do for me?* The catholic: *what can I do for God; what is my mission?*

Me & the Rev were in heated discussion; felt a soft gentle arm reach around me offer a photograph *It's You!* She said—it was Miss Celeste baring a photography of him—*it's from her!* (Indicating the wicked Faye.) — *No No*, Transman pushed it away--*too much drama*. He told her. Meaning about things that once might have connected them as friends—he certainly was not going to receive friendly overtures from the wicked Faye, after her siding w/Hawk; and the evil Hawk just sitting there, crazily, never having uttered a word of apology and libel to do the same thing again after any given period of time… He wanted no more connection to them. No more monstrous drama. And so, after this brief, icy interlude, they went back to their discussions of movie stars, the gossip of the industry idols we know, but they don't know us in return. Stars who gaze out of their penthouse windows at a vast city veiled w/myriad lights—behind every light might be a fan, but who, where, they do not know, —but they are known.

Billions; myriads glistening lights out of the city blink-blink to them.

Yupsters walking up/down Polk Strassa as the gays of yester-year once strolled from Sutter up to Clay & back.

> Well they are funny. It sad. Down deep they are sad. Doing this fun like they want to belong. They have these meet-ups all in the same costume--they want to have fun.
> --Rev Will

The rich trust-fund kids stomped down the street in zig-zag multi colored cloth—packs of eight, ten, fifteen of them; women & men.

They're young—trying to figure out who they are; explore their sexuality.

59

Hawk left soon. Collateral damage, left in her wake; the thin twisted man in the wheelchair now hated him and his crack friends heard all the hateful gossip from the twisted mans mouth--what a cesspool had opened up.

Well when you hit a wall only way to go is up—to ascend.

Homeless still stroll by—dipping into garbage can for left-over food in the process of rotting.

Seniors program—what he needs was a GLBT Seniors—not to be thrown in w/a pack of heterosexual seniors—whose particular age group (over 70) statistically is more anti gay then their middleage or young counterparts.

So many frowns.

Saw so many stores with butcher-block paper, some claim to be closed for remodeling, some will never open. —And gays leaving not just the city, but the state; can't afford the rents.

The lesbian watercolorist says dentists have the highest rates of suicide, and only special insurance companies will carry their policies; some dentists use nitrous oxide for pain control also proven to be carcinogenic, and then, undertakers. Undertakers are risk of a great variety of disease from working w/dead bodies. Also formaldehyde used in embalming is highly carcinogenic.

Told me how she use to inhale nitrous oxide from whipping cream— devices sold in Head Shops that catch up the cream, so you can inhale just the gas.

Nitrous oxide displaces oxygen, which gives you the high. If it displaces too much oxygen it kills you.

Woman who wrote a book auto-gynophyllia; men who get a charge out of being in a woman's body; on surface looking like a woman, dressing like a woman; sexual charge out of that but no desire to be a woman underneath.

Faye has said more then a few times about how he is a man: *underneath all this I'm a man honey.*

Oh, here is the scuttlebutt about that new hospital going up on Van Ness Ave: *I think they're going to do their best to keep out certain people... expect those who can bring the highest profit margin. They want the rich.*

Where Miss Daisy at? Usually expect to see her and was hoping to see her and share a hee-haw & a jaw-jack w/her.

Oh, saw Celeste is back in the company w/Hawk.

PM
Now after talking to Priest Will, am thinking about my goals once more. If it is true I do not have to try to earn Gods approval, God's love—Gods special attention, might I reprioritized my goals? I could go on self-sacrificing, and working endlessly to achieve some magical goal—a high rating w/God... but if this wasn't Her-His will... would I keep on doing that? No... after some thought he realized. *No, if it was actually going contrary to God's will for me, I would stop.*

Emptied liquor bottle lays in flower cauldron.

Sunday, March 10
Cat sits in large flowerpot under the window. Investigates it. Her rump and furry head just fit curled in it. She curls in it. Stands in it. Sits on her haunches in it. Eats some dead leaves out of it. Cat fun.

The walk up to the Cross is a very long distance there are decades of places to stop upon your journey. From the last row to the middle. – might take half a lifetime. From the middle to the front, needs the fixed faith of old age. To the ministry. To the alter. To the choir loft. To the mahogany high backed chairs @ the asp under the large gold crucifix. To the sainthood.

Steps.

Title of next book—steps?

Science is mastering the secrets of the physical universe—in the study of physics. For us to try to imagine the Eternal using the laws of physics is impossible—but to set up a border of which the Eternal *cannot be smaller then it*—in other words, *think outside the box.*

One of the 6-gang rapists of India's Shame has committed suicide in his jail cell. He, like the others is facing the death penalty. Good! Thought this might happen.

The Catholic Church torturous inflexibility derailed the lives of millions of people. My father and his girlfriend a 50-year old widow, his age, whom he'd met @ work —20 years after his failed marriage—from which he had not gotten a divorce. This catholic lady friend was forbidden to marry dad, even after such a lengthy separation from my mother—the insane Jane. Not being able to marry her, nor live w/her full time I'm sure contributed to his early death. So much good could have been done.

Monday, March 11
Rarified hellifications.

A prostitute; large, alabaster white legs & thighs bare; clumsily wobbles on high red high heels down Polk Strassa; now takes off one pump and walks on the other and bare foot with a staggered gait.

The wind was blowing—cold—maybe he should have brought his warm hat w/earflaps.

Went by the 4th Wave coffee shop to say hi to employee woman there to kill time—can't depend on anything in this life. Butcher block paper covering the windows. Closed For Remolding For 2 Weeks.

Met Dr. Sam in Trader Ho's parking lot after shopping. We had a necessary nosh at Sliders, then on to see Oz. Good movie, which was inspiring.

PM
In the Old Testament there are scriptures dealing w/how the Hebrew People's must handle the ark. The great ark houses the scrolls—there are written all the history in Torah, which came earlier then the New

Testament, including centuries of oral tradition—the first 5 books—including the Ten Commandments.

Tuesday, March 12
A beautiful sun shone over the city--& on Coyote. OM sorry he had not applied his sun block as the Eternal had indicated he should—so brief a hint, what non-believers call *intuition*. Sun was back

Talked to bro Leo on the phone; on his way to Dallas TX for Blax Transman Conference.

A homeless mad Chinese comes along vigorously brushing his teeth; foam on his mouth like a rabid-dog —spits into the Owner's garbage can. Hawks, then spits again—what a sight... Ugh.

Removes somebody's crumpled napkins from the trash receptacle and wipes his face w/manic zeal. Then trods on upon his journey.

Saw Cosmo. The old guys sat out there all afternoon, apparently, from about 2—so TM arrived just as the last straggler left.

Joe being released from prison this Sunday—not going to Walden House—a no-drug facility, but utilizing some 3 month program which puts him up in a hotel free and gives him money for food. This sounds like it will be a lot easier for him to start back up on drugs, with this lax system.

Another homeless compatriot stumbling across the street; his body weakened, but only age 40.

Next comes the trans girl who was locked up in a closet age 3 to 13, when she escaped her parents—for being a transgender child.

Here comes lady w/abandon pit bull she has rescued.

The shaky bum ambulating angst. He is sad; he is continually sad. Since a child. Still can't get over how he was treated --then sad! Who would treat a wonderful child so bad? The child knows it and is stuck on sad. From beginning to the end

A little engine goes running along trailing cigarette smoke. Human engine grinding out energy.

A lovely concert about to transpire @ the very edge of the Ho's parking lot– steel guitar – man unpacks amplifier, battery pack; very well planned, plugs in the cords to the guitar. Wonder how long it will take for the officious officials to trot out of the Ho's and threaten him and tell him: *I'm sorry sir, but you must move on.*

Sets up. Takes him about 15 minutes to and now he begins. Music fills the parking lot.

We artists set upon our rarified work.

Brown skin man comes by throws some change into the open guitar case. Scatters; a few coins fall in front on the sidewalk. Woman on bench next to Transman gets up picks up a coin, but instead of going to throw it in the guitar case, she holds it & sits back down. What is she going to do with the coin? That is the question. Chinee.

Well this is the higher road in the situation… that as an artist you put forth your best—to create your God-sent art; but some won't receive it well and some will rob you, but others will be inspired—and your soul has gone out into the world!

Ah! Into the bucket goes the coin. Chinese has politely waited until he finished his song!

Music good; better then good. Voice sadly not great. Maybe after street playing years or so, all will evolve into better.

Why are all of us artists working for spare change?

The sun was now setting into the ocean, West; streaming its gold rays down 50-block length of Bush Street thoroughfare beaming distant light upon the old guy.

PM

You did not know this. I did not know this. Living in semi-warm California, San Francisco. This news is better known in America's North East, and in the Midwest.— Where it gets cold cold at night.

Poor families must spend $2,000 a year to heat their homes during the winter—and we know this is far greater then many poor folks monthly salary.

Hugo Chavez, socialist leader of Oil Rich nation Venezuela down in South America—has an *American* program, which pays for heating oil for 156,000 poor *American* families. He has bought out an American oil company to distribute his Venezuelan oil. Many well-off neighbors are pissed that the poor of our nation are turning to a Communist country for help but as one low-paid working black woman said—*its not about Communist nothing, it's about being cold.* And all must agree, if you are freezing in your home and someone offers to heat it for free, you will gladly accept. One white man said how: *I went to every single American agency and to the American oil companies and none of them would help me.* Then Hugo Chavez helped him and he has spent the last several winters in warmth!

America get a clue!

Rich people get a clue!

Compassion is what it is about! We know people and even animals w/warm fur coats sicken and die in the cold! We need all the amenities of a civilized life!

> Medicine.
> Free of pain.
> Housing.

Wednesday, March 13, 11AM

> We must etch ourselves into the human tableaux using every tool
> possible, or we will be forgotten. Obliterated. Effaced. Our culture
> will swirl slowly down the drain—along with too many other dead
> peoples. A lost tribe. Culture is vital to a tribe's self-identity, pride,
> esteem, and subsequently, their happiness.
> --PASSAGE

Am spell checking beginning text of LIFE BOTTOM OF WORLD, before prepare to go to Shrink.

How can we ever hope to have a good life w/this malefic Sandstone building towering over us; it's cruel policy's grinding over us w/financial servitude; grabbing and greedily stuffing itself, making itself bigger, bigger, while we starve & die?

Bare wood frames stand in space—to 6th story, beyond wind-burgeoning black tarpaulin to protect the units going in underneath.

Shrink.

Feel great. Talked to shrink. Thinking of Amazon sales & complement given to me last week—and poster sales request. Plus something to do tonite. Also promise of the future.

A beautiful clean white grey pigeon flaps away into the sky. So clean & healthy. Is it a fanciers pigeon—who sleeps in a well-heated coop @ night?

Sat across Van Ness Ave in place he use to live 40 years past, which was tore down. Sat in the sun. Glad he had applied his sunblock.

Every large powerful nation on earth has played their turn @ being Empire. How can we blame ours as if it were exceptional? 150 years ago Britain ruled half the nations on earth!

So many citizens in this country have come of age (into their mid 50's) to find the pensions they worked for & once counted on are non-existent.

Out @ Coyote in hot sun.

Grace, Dean's lecture series on Cathedrals.

W/lightening speed a new Pope has been chosen. Francis.

He is a Jesuit. Francis is a name belonging to the Order of Franciscans—who give all their money away to the poor. Jesuits are quite the opposite.
--Dean Jane

The Dean spoke of the rise and fall and fall and rise of Cathedrals all across Europe. In one epoch they chopped heads off of the statues, in another they broke out all the stained glass windows. In another they used Cathedrals to store ammunition & stable their horses.

Black gal w/hoody that reads TUSKEGEE; a black college—where my grandfather graduated and went on to get a high paying job.

Thai food plus Thai iced coffee & fried bananas w/Annie:

I think we are all the same vehicle. We are all the same—you see a car, a bus, a van, a garbage truck—they are all the same vehicle inside different forms. So the lower life forms are the same as us. They have the ability to feel pain & suffering as we do. People treat animals like inanimate objects they totally forget all about it.
--Annie Ho

PM
We have a real serious and important work to do for God—this haggling over abortion, gay rights, women priests, is just a roadblock. It should be clear what is to be done:

--Women's rights over their own bodies
Greater control over the situations that
put women in risk of unwanted
pregnancy
--Poverty
--Women's self esteem
--Women's control over her body in or out
of marriage w/a man

Greater works to be done for God:

Healing
Compassion
Instruction

This is for certain; one following the ministry may think they are sadly unsuited. They may desire first & foremost to follow the Eternal and to do all that the Eternal desires. They may have seen the things of this earth pass away—leaving them empty-handed, which determines them even more to follow the Spirit, instead of flesh.

However they are so poor @ it all—looking back in hindsight how they failed in even the smallest compassions they could have had—to their life mate, to their dogs & cats even.

Well I tell you—despite all this—continue on your path in following the Eternal by all means possible!

For in this all will be added to you. All forgiveness. All instruction. All self-realization. And you will, by the end of this journey be Well Employed!

So discouraging. The newly elected Poop has declared he is against abortion and homosexuality. Well that knocks 2 out of 3 out of the box right away, with no guessing games to be played out over the years. Now, what about women priests?

Once she is pregnant—it is the woman's decision what she does with her body! Well she is bringing forth children say the detractors—who wish to seize this basic power from her. It is just the facts—women are given the gift of being able to conceive and bare children—not men! If men wish to get pregnant and have a baby—without having an abortion, they should do so! But do not interfere with what a woman does with her own body!

Men have already seized practically every power they can away from women—it has taken 5,000 years to begin bringing about equality of the sexes in all walks of life. But some men are not content with running the jobs, running the finances, running the politics, running the holy institutions, running the doctors office, running their mouths—in short being in charge of everything—now they even want to control what a woman does with her body—the same way men controlled slaves! This is what they want! The return of slavery!

Either the intelligent people of earth want freedom, equality, democracy, for all beings w/no exceptions—or they don't! Decide!

Old Transman was thinking about work—work in the garden. Which is a good thing to do. And then he thought about love. The work of love.

Do not ask what is it; let us go and make our visit.

Why is it some chose to check out of this world instead of stay & fight...

For animal rights. Against the abuse of unfeeling human kind. Fight in defense of the heart—of love—over greed.

Thursday, March 13
The OM stopped by a blax-owned art gallery; saw the photographs of Gordon Parks, a well-known blax photographer. Very nice studio in the heart of tourist district. Seeing no black face there he held back his photos (of his paintings) wanting to show them to the lady owner, in person.

He made his way to Grace.

The congregation packs the choir loft, a sea under the asp.

The congregation is all old—grey—this is not good. But for a few children squalling down in the crypt. But non-sufficient to replace the Old Guard. None.

> Red: (Soto Voice) Well that's for sure.
>
> Congregation: (Recites scripture.)
>
> Red: Yeah.
>
> Congregation: (Recites scripture.)
>
> Red: Yeah.
>
> Congregation: (Recites scripture.)

69

Red: Not exactly…

God: *I pick them out--& set them up on high.*

Red: Your Grace endures forever. Give thanks.

The Old Mans mind goes on, elevated from his distaste @ being surrounded by the Old Guard—venture kapitalists & exploiters of yesteryear—inheritors of massive wealth; fortunes; & forgoes his tears of misery—he is inspired!

Saw the Bishop's shining face and wild white wispy hair; the one he had not spoken to @ first, 5 years past when the Bishop began his reign, and he'd seen him downstairs in the crypt, (the OM being such a sensitive snob-in-reverse) but this Bishop, Marc, had proven to have a very high philosophy about saving the environment, the planet, the animals, Women's Rights and other holistic stuff, so he was pleased w/said Bishop.

Jesus fucken' shit. He thought. It was sobering fact. *Jesus fucken' shit.*

On to the dinner. A throng well over 100-souls. Barely a blax or colored face among them. Noshes abounded in food-mountains over 4 tables.

So much emotion attached to their money.

> I have traveled to the 88 churches in our diocese and am seeing in
> the pews not the rich patrons as is supposed of our church, but
> many who don't have jobs, who have been out of work 2, 3, years,
> who are loosing their homes.
> --From Bishop Marc

Then the Bish testified to the great job the church budget managers have done:

> The auditors, planning commissions. They have saved for us not in
> the thousands, not in the hundreds of thousands, but in the millions
> of dollars.

Annie continues her diatribe against the first church she knew, in her childhood, the Born Again Evangelical Chinese Christians; says their hatred of gays has fucked everybody up—not just gay people— but anybody associating w/them, their families, friends. Years of misunderstanding.

PM

Remembering back our conversations, Annie & Wayne @ Chinese restaurant—Paul's letters, New Testament. Wayne somehow tries to explain; says how God has created each of us w/a work in mind, for us to do for Her-His world. So we find our mission in the knowledge of that.

Thinking about needles, about doses; sitting on sidewalk in the alley back to a brick wall *veinly* trying to stitch themselves back together again.

Friday, March 15

Everybody is a creation of psychology. An individual, one is raised knowing they are an endangered species. Others have no realization, only they are part of a large group of people who like each other and are content, happy: *people just like me—I like them and they like me.*

Which community will be strongest?

The foolish children (age 20's) are playing their games of the privileged on Geary Boulevard. Faces smeared w/pink warpaint. Consulting their $600 I-pods: *Mission and 4th next? No Ellis & Taylor*—on a cyber treasure hunt.

The panhandlers are short. No cigarettes no coins.

PM

Am afraid & apprehensive. Letter from the Food Stamp office. This is so horrible. How can a government oppose its own people? It is eating us up from the inside out. It all needs to be changed, overhauled.

They measure out grants to us—but turn a blind eye against unbridled capitalism. In other words landlords own our houses instead of we

71

the people each owning our own domicile. The government measures out a few dollars of food, but the rent increases in giant gouges yearly—our Social Security pensions are not keeping pace. How can the wretched food stamps gouge us for eating into our food grant—when we have barely enough to stay alive after paying this horrifying rent?

Comrade Fidel Castro gave each Cuban citizen a free place to live. What a blessing that is! How many of the poor here would love that. Just talked to hard-working Grace professional (law) who has been unemployed in her old age:

> My Social Security pays my rent w/$20 left over per month. How am I suppose to live on $20?

> You are in the same boat as a lot of us. I'm piecing my rent together from Social Security, help from Grace, and my Amazon sales. Then its paid. For food I have food vouchers and food stamps but they are steadily trying to cut those.

We are like gods. We are imitators of God. We are ducklings who follow their mothers and chicks who learn from their hen; a child who is taught by its mother & father; to learn and grow up to be an adult society. This is how we learn from God.

Saturday, March 16
I was awoken w/a interesting dream. Many symbols were given. A triangle, made of white lines, was demonstrated. Some how it had power—aimed @ the head for uttermost effect.

I was not sure where this teaching came from. If it was a mysticism, but not from Jesus I cannot employ it.

Outside.

People in green come walking along. Green caps, green shirts, green dresses, green high heels, green tiaras…

Oh ma gawd; he suddenly realized it was St. Patrick day—

72

Great deal of folk (mostly young). Walking—green hats which said: *I'm Irish & I'm Drunk!* Etc. Marching back to Powell Street on a mission.

Coyote; sat in sun w/Henny & his old gay friend…young people keep up a youthful ruckus across the street, and parades of them march to/from the coffee shop here. The youth are in the 20-year age bracket.

Up & down youth in green parade, shouting, laughing; women screaming, laughing hysterically, snorting…

Across Polk Street the two taverns have 3 security guards in blue uniform w/SECURITY written across the back and a police squad car has now parked and an officer joins them. They are to guard the revelers.

Affluent youth, tourists from out of town they have made their way up the hill from the Irish St Patrick Day parade down on Market Street.

Affluent youth being picked up by private ZZZ chauffer service, and the pink moustache livery service.

Terra green pea pennants from the St Paddy's day parade.

Reminds me of my dear friend/crony Irish Lassie Katherine Rhealmen, about whom I wrote one of my longest novels:

> So the days trickled on at the wireroom, like music wandering aimless with no purpose, a jazz with no faith, meandering until it gets into trouble.
> --WestPoint Of The Universe

Knowledge is good but God is better.

> Knowledge is good so you won't be such a fool.
> --The Malaysian

Shouts & music grinds out of taverns; war woops, and yells.

In America—a lot of loneliness. In the old country you still have the old customs—family. Even if you hate your family you can depend on them.

If you have nothing else at least you have your family.

The crowd has grown 5 times larger. 4-cops now. They are herding the tumult of green wearing youth back down the street to contain them in front of their two taverns. So they don't go meandering off thru the neighborhood, lost, wreaking havoc.

Spent more time talking in the Ho's parking lot, in sun until it went down, and no gold light remained.

PM
Nice talk w/the Malaysian; see we are friends again.

Historic vote of 200 nations taken in UN @ New York—unanimously passed bill to appose violence towards women globally:

> In combat zones
> In domestic relationships

10 years ago this same bill failed to pass the UN because many nations were not willing to oppose violence in domestic relationships. Now after all the horror of rape and murder against wives, women, has steadily emerged, they think differently. Passing this historic bill.

> We can't survive half democracy half oligarchy any more then we can survive half slavery half free.
> --Bill Moyers

Moyers said how he came from a poor family; his friend came from a rich one. But they both went to the same public high school, played in the same public park & went on to the same public state university and were well educated and went on to have good lives.

Today, the middle class is shrinking and the poor have been left behind. The schools are becoming privatized. It is much harder for a poor or middleclass child to reach their dream.

Well, Life @ The Bottom Of The World of course—means people on the very lowest echelon who sleep in blankets on the street, beg money for cooking oil, PU sticks of wood or cow dung for fuel and can afford only a handful of rice to cook 1 evening meal—all they have to eat all day; who are skin/bones.

Let me tell you the story of it still another time. This is from a excellent short story which appeared in the New Yorker or some-such 'zine, written by an ethnic Indian writer—or Indonesian or someplace very very po'. The story went like this:

> We are introduced to a family in destitution who live in a shack constructed of several wooden pallets set up on some large stones, w/flimsy walls and a tin roof—it is about 8 feet by 16 feet square. Their shack is side-by-side w/hundreds of others, similar, and 2 feet outside runs a drainage ditch, which runs with sewage. The dying father sleeps in one corner on a blanket; two young children, a girl & boy go out to beg daily, the mother tends their home. She goes out to get water; stands in line @ single water faucet for 300 people. An older daughter works as a prostitute, she lives in town. Often the children come home w/so little that the mother, instead of buying food sends her young son out to buy a chemical dope, sold cheaply, an inhalant in a recycled can which all the family huffs and it slacks their hunger for hours. ---Drugs. They drink soup made out of water. On this particular day the prostitute daughter returns home for a visit—driven by a wealthy client who pulls up in front of the shack in the muddy sewer in his fancy polished car. The family hugs and kisses—they really love each other and miss older sister. She has brought them several bags of groceries. The family tears into the packages, happily yanking out item after item gorging themselves on food. So much so that they vomit later—from excess. The family can only spend a few hours together before the wealthy client returns to pick up the daughter. She is barely 20, young, thin; she is dying of HIV AIDS. One day she will be too sick to return to them. The family will have no more respite of delicious food. And they will mourn for their lost sister.

Sin cannot survive in the presence of God. It is because sin is a mistake. God is perfect. When sin comes in contact w/God, God's power & goodness can't help but release sin back into goodness—the

75

mistake is dissolved ending its psyche 'existence'. Sin is conquered, dismissed, released; the person is now free of their affliction.

Sunday, March 17

> So much of the world---has well masked—its lament—either individual, or collective. Noise is so pervasive. Humans are afraid of silence. Thus its competitive and can't hear each individual cry.
> -Priest Andy Loban from Lucy Winkett

How we silence sounds, voices of pain so to contain them, —while not stifling the person.

Tonite I was lector 1, church.

PM
Nice evening after service: Wayne, Annie H. & me. (No this is not Mr. Wayne from then men's sex theatre—I gave the lad that name, now am stuck w/2 Wayne's, the real one & the nom-de-plume.)

Again, pictured someone from church in my mind's eye— simultaneously a SQUAWK from white; in her cage in kitchen.

Monday, March 18
He spent the day seated in Dentists office watching Native American Close circuit TV w/health advice including nutrition tips. All black haired tan Native Americans.

Before the Old Man got to Coyote, saw @ bus stop the Olde Pervert. They began a rip roaring discussion about hooker Joe, who was suppose to have been released Sunday:

> Well he didn't call me.

> He didn't call me either.

> He knows I want to see him.

> Well he knows I don't have any money.

> Well I've been seeing this young man w/tattoos.

76

@ this point a young man seated next to them in the kiosk w/2
friends, —they were lighting up marijuana in a pipe— who had been
listening to this sleazy conversation said:

>Pardon me sir, did I hear you say you like young boys?

>Yes, have you got any?

>Yes, this friend of mine does that… do you want to write your
>phone number on this paper for me?

>I don't know.

Then the bus came and engulfed all of them.

Red was soon seated @ the tan lacquered wooden counter which ran
along the plate glass window of Coyote, facing Polk Strassa—his
window seat.

In the tavern across the street, the wood panel mural is progressing;
the artist has painted in arms, legs, drinkers in a microcosm bar—skin
tones; bottles of liquor line the background. Men in blue shirts black
coats; flesh tones. Blue, red bolts of color.

So weary—from getting ready for dentists & nerve pill; from worries
about letter from the government foodstamps/medical care.

Coyote played flowery, frolicking music reminiscence of a ballet
studio or art school.

Their eyes, be they opened.

6PM. Coyote closing early; tables & chairs all going inside. The
owner is feeling sick.

PM
Hideous communiqué from government—cutting off my medical care
and my food stamps I must pay $150 per month—because 2 Bancroft
checks came in back to back and makes it look like I earn over $1,500
per month—which is a lie.

What hell.

Number of social worker ready to call tomorrow.

Tuesday, March 19
The artist paints painstakingly continues the work; right hand up &
now paints a side on the panel.

Am sick. Fighting this cold w/decongestants—speed. And small bites
of Vikoden, or small Ibuprofen. Cold retreating—leaving me
exhausted.

Am so stressed & afraid—of this summons on my desk saying they
are cutting me off my medical insurance and I have to pay them $600!
Where is that money? I never had any money! All my expenses are
documented—they are not extravagant—but for $1,085 monthly rent.
And there is nowhere cheaper to live in the city!

These social workers who get paid to misread your results and kick
you off the program. They count on an atrophy of people who can't,
won't, fight any longer, and forgo the stupid stamps.—Thus saving
them money.

Hateful. Despicable. Unspeakable.

PM

> Creation is in travail, birth pains, waiting for the world to be born.
> --1 Corinthians, or Romans

> Very very very dapper blax man on corner super clean, perfectly
> fitted tan slacks zoom pipe stem legs, matching vest; bowtie deep
> crimson red, same red as the designer bag he carries—very
> continental leather Italian shoes. He be clean tall sissy? Casually
> holds between 2 effete fingers expensive shopping bag from ultra
> chic boutique; hails a cab—its horrible to think he might spend
> some time out here on this corner and not be picked up—compared
> to other races/shades; worse even to think he might be a criminal
> disguised and be picked up just to pull out a small handgun from
> his elegant coat and rob the cabby.

Just re-read this passage and thought of some of the robbers I know. One, in 1975, from the crowd of us who hung out in black soul club Mr. Bojangles, a black bulldagger murdered a cabbie @ gunpoint. All I remember is was s/he was gone. Gone up for a long time. By the time s/he could have been up for release on good behavior, the whole scene was gone—blown away—the black nite club, all the people. Decades had passed, spare paper blew in the doorway on a street of derelict bums—and the former club remained this way for ten years until a whole new group, affluent dot commies came to town injecting money into the economy for themselves to use SF as a playground.

Wednesday, March 19
If you weren't morally compromised…

Thing sex workers tell you what they like in a person the most is when they *not treating them as a sex worker*. What they want is to have a friend.

Going up to Grace tonite—see what I will be taught.

This early afternoon Spirit of the Lord talked to me; about 3 hours ago I'd prayed: *God don't let me be so afraid.* God came back w/my anger—to control it. And then the word Tolerance. (Tolerincia).

Transactions w/the Eternal.

OM on medication sat in the window seat until he go to Grace & learn (& pray).

A great clearing up –all that oppose you.

Am jittery, jumpy.

Crazy street denizen, walks around w/bewildered expression on his face; walks in the liquor store, out moments later, tips something up— then tossed it to the street—a shorty bottle of brown liquid—liquor— whisky. A 1-shot bottle.

People walking along talking to make-believe friends.

79

Cathedrals are designed to survive the fickleness of fortune, the ups/downs of the culture that surrounds them.
--Pr. Jude Harmon

Something about being in a large space. A small person in such a big space sees *its not all about me, but my place in its vast entirety.* Where I fit in, belong, inside this extensive machinery.

Spiritual but not religious.

Thursday, March 20
In Castro Mission—Rebecca, case facilitator.

Blax man comes out door, heaves a massive sigh—can only be angst of a gay man, worn out by so much crap of this jive-ass system.

The Old Man was living in fear—he was afraid they were stealing his money—but he didn't have any money.

Some jobs I would not work. —Being a negative case investigator who unearths a missing $17 of the government's precious money. My caseworker puts it: *They want to keep you eating their government cheese, and never thrive.* I wouldn't lock up some simple fool for understating $17 a month petty income—but the agents of Hell Food Stamps—have discontinued my grant for that!

$140 ticket for $2! Declares a blax sistah in the street. Fine for being on the bus without a TX. *If you can't get $2 for busfare, they you ain't got $140 for a fine! Does that make sense? The black & whites--- they gotten worse.*

Searching man on the corner. Man in custody. Looking sideways at everybody.

Met w/brother Baz, fun; treated me to breakfast @ Orphan Andy's, gay men (the staff) hissy arguing there; life-giving scrambled eggs w/Swiss cheese; hamburger patty, cold slaw, toast (forbidden), water & coffee.

Click click.

80

Smile! Don't look like a pervert!

What! I am a pervert!

SF is a spiritual stronghold.

Blax street man comes in Laundromat, unpleasant; looks around—
what is he going to do. Transman had to stop reading his newspaper
to turn around & watch to make sure the man didn't steal his laundry
detergent (donated) nor plastic laundry sacks. Man looking for what
he can get. Nerve-racking.

On Phone talked to thin photographer –artist woman from Grace
Seniors. She is 2 quarters shy of Social Security because she was a
teacher in catholic school and they didn't pay into it. Hence her scope
is more limited. Social Security has more leeway. They watch SSI
people more closely, monitor for offenses.

PM
Nada.

God soon is going to come gather up all the loose ends which didn't
work out—into a new thing.

To find God you start @ the crossroads junction of 2 lines…

Friday, March 22
Journey along the road—see some chain smoking; living high, from
one peek blast of crack/crank to the next.

People are fighting, or they are dying.

People give a lot to the world who may not be recognized in their
lifetime. Van Gough inspires multimillions of people; his great
works, and his life struggle. The red-haired bearded man w/piercing
blue eyes wanted desperately for friends, but drove all the few he
made away from himself. Common village children threw stones @
him as he walked thru the town square carrying his easel, and paints,
out into the fields to paint.

Sun beat down on the OM's face. He wrote. He was lonely—for companions—but not so lonely as to sit around corner w/the vicious-tongue Hawk & young man whom fate had twisted into a wheelchair.— Who sat also w/cronies, but @ separate table, since neither one of them wee speaking to each other. The lesbian transsexual sat @ the opposite end of the café, far far away from any of them, doing her watercolors; also alone—and highly engaged.

Queers.

Our life. Its scary.

Grace. Stations Of The Cross.

Again the Old Man sat @ Thai table facing starry night outside the clean plate glass windows; waiting for Param w/peanut sauce, & Annie, who came running across from Chinee restaurant catty-corner baring 2 orders Milk Cakes!

PM
Nada.

Saturday, March 23
Met w/bro Leo @ Coyote. Told me about his adventure in Dallas, Tex in the 2nd annual Black Transman Conference. 100 blax transmen plus wives, girlfriends, transwoman, and supporters, blax, plus some Latins & whites in attendance. He had a wonderful week down there in a fabu hotel.

Saw Celeste in front of Coyote, she greeted me warmly, she sitting w/Hawk & the evil, now-unspeaking Faye, said: *you and I have no problem w/each other*, and I agreed this is true—so here we sit, separated by something dumb. The sun had been faint, but it came out fully hot for about an hour. Leo & I talked & funned. Lady w/dog came past & sat w/us awhile.

I wonder where my future is going, and my work. Thankful to Hashem for bringing me this far—and almost 100 books now! And nearing 20-Spiritual Journals.

Am suppose to meet w/Leo up @ Grace—film some more of YOU TUBE me talking docs. My first done by bro Baz—Nobody's People.

Leo treated me to wonderful brisket of beef/mashed potato dinner @ Hebrew deli. He happily enjoyed the Latkes. Hebrew soul food.

PM
Arguing w/very strong person—they may be wrong, in fact, but their desire for dominance will not let them back down. So a wrong is committed. Once the truth comes out, this wrong backfires against the wrong doer—and their followers. It is this desire for dominance, which complicates the matter of right/wrong.

Sunday, March 24
A lot of people in SF play a little bit of the hustler—because SF is not an ordinary city. Like me, they may have come here as an ordinary person, working in an ordinary city—working @ minimum wage, having sub ordinary expectations—but suddenly the city burgeoned into a very different place, an affluent destination for the rich & you've spent a lifetime here & are being priced out—as a consequence you are hanging on.

The sun nourished him; high in the sky—blazing heat into the OM's bones; listened to fine blax music in the jungle of the Owners gardens; outdoor benches of Coyote.

Well this is so ridiculous one sits on one side of café—devoid of people & the Hawk around the other side—also devoid of people.

Be of a higher mind---says the Lord(ess).

Oh here is a funny. Well apparently this old guy from the Seniors, J, who never worked a day in his life & thus has absolutely no Social Security—only SSI, (Aid to the Disabled, ((tho he was able-bodied)) sits in the bible study always lambasting the American way and preaching communism. And claims Jesus Christ was actually a communist, and that we should recognize Jesus' communism when we see it and etc; and this guy is speaking badly about the American system of kapitalism…

So now in his old age, this American system has provided J with SSI benefits to keep a roof over his head, regardless of the fact he didn't work a day in his life—and giving him free food.

> He's running down kkkapitalism while he's enjoying every minute of it.
> --The Malaysian

An ordinary city, which SF was at the time, at least on the surface—disregarding it's most interesting history; and flushing all non-affluent down the sewer.

Missed church today because there is no 6PM evening service, only the 11AM, Palm Sunday—which spills out onto the steps of the cathedral, it becomes so crowded—which displaces me, a regular attendee.

PM
Some brilliant news has come out of the Philippians. A youthful entrepreneur has invented a solar light made out of a recycled bottle and a piece of tin. It can light a poor favlella dwellers shack for 1 year for only $10 —cost & instillation. It is spreading across the slums, and is going into Asia & Africa. This new invention, household lighting for day/night on the cheep is saving millions of carbon footprints across our environment as well.

Must tell you a bit about today in the sun—an ongoing dialogue w/the Olde Pervert—the other day as usual I sat in the sun, he came by at his usual time after his shop closed, and while we talked, he was approached by a medium size Caucasian man w/dark hair who said he'd just got out of the penitentiary. He was a hustler, and later he and the Olde Jolly got together and dated –it took them 2 hours, for just $20 I believe, unless he is lying.

Well today Old Jolly came by and we shared a few yuk yuks jaw jacking, and he said more about the guy, who frankly resembles Joe a little. He is a bit of interest to me as well. He is older by the way. Neither of us are sure if he is an addict or what. Not sure what he just got out of jail for.

His teeth are bad.

84

So is Joe's—but he can afford false teeth.

He is big. I said, stop when you get to the tonsils.

Oh, due to the fact it is Palm Sunday, some passerby's —walked by carrying green palms.

Big green frond palms wave in the sunny air.

Monday, March 24
A lot of these girls & teenage women are seeing reality thru male lens—cartoons, films, rock music—these have male heroes, male leads, and I guess the woman is suppose to find her place in it— egoless, fitting into the TV drama, which is not hers.

HEY RED! Old Man turned about—sun going in/out on Polk Street in front of the Coyote jungle of plants in gold cauldrons, and park benches—it was Cosmo in his truck DID YUH SEE JOE? HE'S OUT! I JUST DROPPED HIM OFF!

The Old Man was hungry. He had misjudged his budget & would have no money until end of the week—he'd called all his friends & they were gone—or asleep. Sun went in/out @ Coyote it was only 4:30 but young baristas were carrying the parklet benches indoors. No Joe; no Olde Jolly. *Nade de turbe, nada de falta. Those who seek God will never go wanting--* a poor guitarist sat in a picnic chair down the frontage of the café—playing badly—chords, plunks. They were all artists, he and Red, they were all destitute, they all inhabited a narrow space.

OM had $3.65 cents to his name what food could he procure @ the Hos?

The air grew quiet... —The guitarist had gone. It had sounded better when he was playing.

The OM knew he had been stupid to put all his money prematurely into the OCR document—COLLECTED POETRY OF RED JORDAN AROBATEAU, 1 —from his Grace beneficence, and run flat out of

85

cash for 3 more days until Bancroft hits, or $30 worth of Amazon payments hit… but he was not stupid to channel all his energy to writing all these books—100, and paint his 60-80 paintings—not stupid, but very smart!

Filled a verbal complaint about the Hos samples man who never ever said hello to him, but had said, he could not have any more samples after the first 2---it was rude. *I am a customer in here every day on my EBT food card, and I think because I'm poor and a person of color he's typecasting me. He has never said hello to me, he picks and chooses who he says hello to, and only thing he ever says to me is don't take any more samples—so I'm complaining!*

The OM's eyes traveled back/forth searching for stray coins, misplaced fruits or sandwich's. He had already found that day 2 dimes, several pennies and a red apple. Also for the free newspaper out of the battered racks—for birdcage liners.

The streets had been plucked clear—but not of NOTES, of that was aplenty of art—abundant.

The Transman figured he had fucked his own self up—he had no one but himself to blame. Spending $42 on OCR for ebook—which he would not have time to edit for months!

He could be eating delicious food on that $42 now! & not having to steal toilet paper from the Grant Writing Center! (A modest amount.)

The human mechanism is both good & evil. Nice kids—but evil side within them, their friends, their situation draws them into their animalistic nature—when the wheels start really rolling down the wrong track there is a lifetime to pay. White supremacist kids who murdered a migrant worker—3 paid. The most mild-appearing boy got drawn into it. The first kid got 12 to 25 years—he threw rocks at the Migrant. But he did not return later like the other two. The 3 left after the initial attack—laving the migrant laying in the underpass where he had dwelled & slept. The first went home. The other two took methamphetamine then returned to continue their attack, chiefly by pelting the injured migrant w/stones. The second got 25 years to life. But the third—the mildest one, the one who followed and never led—he threw a concrete block at the man's head which outright killed him. Otherwise the man might have survived. This kid got life in prison with no possibility of parole.

City Hall and health department, and the city skyscrapers sit like child's play blocks.

God bless America!! Hebrew brother A. Kaufman reached into his wallet and handed me a crisp $10 bill! Made BofA last withdrawal good, & added food for tonite!

Later Annie called, and we dined!

I have been saved by friends.

In a loud & frantic voice the young Chinese lurched her missive thru the air—on compassion—why the Marriage Equality bill is so important!

PM
Let me make brief summery of what happened today. I was poor & overdrawn @ bank I feared, having no money for food, but $3.

Annie spoke of compassion. She speaks this so often.

Tuesday, March 24
Times they are a changing. Two burly workers converse @ curb: *my half brother, he just came out of the closet last week.* Well yuh know decade ago he would have been prejudicially set against queers, and would have disowned his own brother w/hate.

People pass by the other way, but God stops.

Saw the cat lady @ her accustomed place, begging in the streets—she has succeeded in making an appointment to see the Operative @ Grace tomorrow! Success!

God stops for you & you! No matter what!

Talked w/gay older guys @ Coyote in hot sun. Joe is out of jail and housed in a nice hotel on Market Street. Clean, no bugs. Bathroom down the hall. The state provides it for him for 3 months. In this time he can get on GA, and get food stamps. If he stays clean, he has another program he can access which will give him a free hotel for life—plus medical & food stamps. He can have a life. Maybe my prayer has worked!

Penny ate all her food today; this makes me very happy.

The old guys speak of their medical problems. All of them have diabetes. All but me. They all have cars, is this something to do w/it? My constant walking? We all have big fat guts, some not as large as mine.

Spoke to the lesbian transwoman—she lifted her head a moment from her watercolors to speak, we agreed many of the hustling men here are all jailbirds and seem to have compromised IQ's. So what else can they do w/their lives? In a city like this where you have to be smart and fast to work even the minimum wage coffee shop jobs.

> They all just got out of the penitentiary and have spent their life going in & out of jail, their IQ is about the same as their shoe size, they are all worthless losers.

It was interesting to hear her speak of being a troubled teen who had great difficulty learning in school because of mental disturbances—PDST and ADT (Attention Deficit Disorder). And my self too, I said, at age 14, how I was struggling just to sit in the seat and stay in the classroom—much less hear anything; impossible to learn a single thing—since I considered it a victory that I'd just been able to sit in the seat during the class—our mental problems weren't discussed, kids are just herded into a classroom and expected to go thru all the steps—but how I had turned my disorders into a victory having achieved in my art—tho not yet famous nor rich, but I have Done It! A victory!

The sun was fleeting fast out of the sky—now the sun too deserted human kind—due to our misdeeds? The sun not wanting to shine upon us in disgust?

The wind blew.

88

The sun—going in/out in variegated sky grey/white billows over Cathedral turret into the plaza.

Grace. Helped prepare food for tomorrow din @ Crosby hotel; me so tired. Peeled potatoes, apples, cut cauliflower, chopped apple slices.

It was time for the Old Man to sit down—after standing 2 hours straight, & uphill march before that. His hips hurt as never before. Had not stood that long for decades. Rest.

The food is dependant on the food bank of course. No cheese. Hot dogs for meat.

Cooked for the free meal @ Grace Episcopal services SRO hotel. Not enough meat for my tastes—tried to tell the boss cook that, but dared not be too impolite. They put a lot of franks back into the freezer— easily could have cooked twice as much.

The thing about these SRO hotel dwellers—none of them are vegetarians! I have served @ both SRO hotels for 3 years and know this very well—none of them are vegetarians! They are formerly low-class, street dwellers—and they are meat eaters! They think like me—that they need meat to keep their bodies running!

I had to cheat and sneak back to the kitchen and pick extra meat out of the wonderful casserole so I had enough meat on my plate!

Thank God Bancroft coming tomorrow I believe.

My friends really helped me out last nite—and am thankful---Alan Kaufman reached into his wallet and gave me a $10—I was so flat broke-needed it. And kind Annie took me to Chinese food (including Milk Cakes) so was saved on Monday—and this Tuesday is a breeze and Wednesday too—Bancroft may have arrived then, but at least by Thursday when Amazon too is due!

Must not get the OCR prematurely again. Will wait until the next Bancroft for it!

PM

TV program about hippy lifestyles—living back on the land. Dropping out of the grid of the rat race.

Conscientious poverty.

> To turn evil to good. Hate to compassion. I believe in the power of good, of compassion, but its no good without action.
> --Jewish Woman Auschwitz survivor

My father had obesity & my mother had mental illness—I have a trace of both of it—I have escaped the dragon, but am licked by the dragon's breath.

Wednesday, March 27

Owner came out of the kitchen—saw T's Cheetos on the counter beside his steaming coffee. *He didn't pay for these-- Ring them up!*

He did pay for it! Cries the barriesta.

What a mean man!

T had paid. Reaching into his pocket once for the coffee, and a second time for the Cheetos—a total of $3!

The Owner is distraught, frustrated, wild overworked... whatever.

Henny stopped coming in there, he says the Owner has gotten rude, mean. He wasn't like that before. After all these years of giving him good business, he deserves better. He won't come in.

The other owner is so nice. *How are you tonight sister?* He says— this habit of gay men to call each other sister backfires on a transman who has struggled a lifetime to project their male identity! Oh well!

One word came to the OM's mind when he thought of Olde Jolly— who would retreat back upstairs to his apartment—and the only men to call him want money—the word is *empty.*

The OM was overjoyed. He rejoiced! His money had come in! He was so happy!

90

The American flag furls red/white/blue stripes & stars fading into the mist of SF fog, atop a high tower. Waiting PU Dr. Sam.

Saw Scottish lady w/whom food server at the Grace SRO's:

> I am going to court—they are trying to evict me from my apartment.
>
> It never was like this before.
>
> I know.
>
> I got here in '67 it wasn't like this.
>
> I got here in '81, it wasn't like this. I've seen it change.
>
> I'd like to see it end but I don't think it will.
>
> I'd like to see it end & I think it will end.
>
> I'm with you.

PM
Good Lord! Communiqué from Grace! *Grace cathedral is flourishing is due, in no small part to your financial support!*

AURRGH! Then the cathedral is sinking fast! If it is dependant on my financial support!

The Old Man in sheer terror had isolated those words!

> The world belongs to the people. 7 billion people, not religious despots or royal families. The idea of rule by, Kings, Queens, any religious dictator or, despots are passed into history. They are outdated.
> --His Holiness, 14th Dali Lama of Tibet

Thursday, March 28
T-Man sat in blazing sun between 3 species.—Human, dog, pigeon. Human stood w/their dogs on leash, 4 foot, brown fur coat—pink

tongue lolling, eyes bright. Pigeon flaps; swoops across street; well-fed, feathers luxuriant, held up by air.

An attractive white woman, blond, stands between 2 parked cars in alley, pulls down trousers to her ankles, @ her crotch a thong bikini—her white naked flesh—she is taking a wiz.

All the little tiny elements a person's world is composed of; minor interactions, which encourage, or tear you down.

The lowest wage-earners in the city deal in recyclables (metal, bottles, plastic) for cash—in their zeal, (a grand zeal) to prevent this substandard financial action, the Hos creates a garbage receptacle for its parking lot w/tiny holes to police their garbage—so the frantic indigent recyclers can't easily dig, forage thru their trash for metal/glass/plastic. Alors! Also, no room for shoppers to put trash into it! They have to leave larger trash *beside* the can! Further, due to the rounded shape of the receptacle's top (another efficiency) can't place the too-large trash on top of it. Garbage slides off of it to the pavement. —So into the street it goes! HA HA HA HA! Cheap-ass bastards!

It is said what you want God to do for you should do to others & fortuitous events transpire. T had great debate w/the Eternal just whose words were the words of his JOURNEY journal --his & God's together, or God's alone, or entirely his words alone! These words of the journals, whose thoughts were they? Gods!

All will be restored.

Cross gone! He entered the cathedral—turned to bow to the Cross, as was his custom—the Cross is draped in cloth! All the prayer candles in the little sand box—gone. The cathedral is cold, harsh, still…

Disrobed for white vestments; or according to their Order—purple robes.

Foot washing basins, gone, chairs carried off; candles extinguished. Candle sticks gone.

Chairs being removed off the bema; a parade of worker ants carrying off the stage set, piece by piece.

@ top of the cathedral to 60 foot high, evening's last light faded from behind stained glass windows towering to the North.

His body in so much pain, & cold, hungry.

Now the exodus begins; remaining chairs, all holy clothes; rustling of green palms— gone. Overhead lights gone out—.

Changing. Season to season.

Candles removed. Candlesticks walk off of the bema. Alter clothes folded, taken away, the padded kneelers… carried by two priests each…

Looks like the church was moving. Clearing-out day. The draped crucifix hung in space like a ghost.

Felt a little foolish bowing to a draped ghost crucifix.

PM
Communion w/the sacred.

This monstrous malevolent sandstone building; this money, this consent venture kkkapitalists w/grandiose plans to make more money and more money and more and more and more and more money & grind over people & grind & grind us until we dead or removed out.

Yet one fact historical must be remembered—these grandiose powers do grind on for a time, for a long time—and then they break. Helter skelter they explode their minions all over the place—they fall!

Friday, March 29
Must tell you am anxious—cut off my medical coverage. Am too lonely & w/out romance; suffering lack of success & now medical benefits cut off because my income is too great! —Yet it is not enough to pay my rent & eat! I am still eating replated food found atop garbage cans!

PM
The Valley Of Dry Bones—my reading for the Great Vigil Saturday night!

Saturday, March 30
Coyote. Sun blazing.

Saw Joe! Handsome! Buff, the young man strode across the street, and soon was beside the Old Man; gave him a hug.

Muscular chest stretching out his white teeshirt. Black leather jacket.

Red felt Joe's back, it was thick, solid; he had been working out in prison:

> I'm going to stay clean. I'm going back to trucking school to get my C-3 license. I can drive. I'm going to stay clean.

The young man then encountered one of his vulnerable young dope-addict friends, slender, female, blond; and they walked off together. I hope he can stay strong—and not be led back down the slope of drugs by drug friends.

Saw Cosmo a short time later, w/his new boy toy, another challenged youth of the streets, looks like he is a lower mentality; very nice:

> Joe told me he's going to stay clean. He's enrolled in NA, and he's going to get GA and foodstamps. He told me the only reason why he went back on drugs was he didn't have a place to stay.

The OM agreed. He had seen Joe asleep in a cardboard box on a rainy night. He had seen the futility of Joe turning a $60 date, spending the whole amount on a low-cost hotel room for one night, and having to do this night after night—there was no hope of staying housed that way, thus an easy slide into escape—drugs, the alleys, the gutters. W/this new prison-program, he was housed and could get his feet situated on solid ground.

Joe certainly looked handsome! In white teeshirt, black leather jacket, and bluejeans:

94

I got in a fight and lost all my stuff. I lost the envelope w/your address. I hoped you'd write again.

I didn't want to write again not having any money to send you. Didn't want you to be disappointed.

I lost your phone number. I lost everything.

My prayer has worked, and I told him:

All of us want you to stay clean. You look great.

We all have our weaknesses. The OM realized his. Tho he had conquered alcohol, drugs, & tobacco, and was wrestling w/obesity— he still had not conquered nostalgia, nor disappointment, nor sadness about not being in a relationship. He was needy, as the saying goes.

He admired Joe's strong body and wanted to date him—to fuck him. But knew you cannot possess another humanbeing, nor guarantee they will stay in your corner. So we must all be individually strong. And being a child challenged in his youth by loss of his mother, this was a lesson the poor Old Man had not learned well enough!

He sat outside Coyote café, drinking coffee & speaking with the Malaysian. Soon it was time to go. The fog had swallowed up the sun, & it might rain. He encountered Cosmo @ the end of the block, w/his new trade—the inside of his truck was full of backpacks. And he explained how all that stuff went underneath, and the whole thing turned into a bed, and he had curtains which he fastened on the windows—and drove out into a niche in the shoreline park—for privacy, to have sex.

Certainly is better then paying $60 for a crappy hotel room—w/bugs!

There was @ least one older lady out there—panhandling lady dressed in fine leathers, attractive middle age—an alcoholic—she says:

95

He sure is a handsome man, but they are a dime a dozen. Men like him are all over the place. Young; I'd prefer you over him—wisdom.

Well someone appreciates me!

PM
Practicing my reading for tonite—the Great Vigil.

Red felt bad that he had no money and could not proposition Joe. His budget had assumed primacy in his life—and was working on the next Bancroft shipment, from which he might spare $40—but that would not happen for 2 more months! He dare not risk any extravagance!

What is all this madness about charging money for sex? Can't figure it out! One day I might have a lot of money—due to the art… what will life be like then? Real? Or a trick?

Off to Grace!

Nite vigil! Shadows! Dark! Fire burns in the firepit! Hundreds of parishioners mill about in the darkness! Our Savior is in hell! Dead, descended to the depths!

Resurrection!

The OM felt inadequate—felt like taking drugs himself to bolster himself from his fear of HIV, fear of rejection, fear of loneliness, fear of homelessness; wandering in a big city.

Beautiful sky white puff clouds over blue—pink tinge! Birds fly. Sunset. Shine brilliantly against flat facing of downtown skyscrapers shining hundreds of thousands of square feet of office windows

Oil princess getting married. Heiress to vast oil fortunes of Saudi Arabia, in upscale Fairmont hotel.

Click click; snap snap snap; tourists capturing pictures of Grace cathedral, Camera's focus; light flashes over her gothic face in an instant bolt of lightening.

Acerbic smell; fire burnt from the earlier service. Lights are out. The Old Man went down the corridor to the vestry where they had all been summoned; mounting 4 marble steps—once back there he was *called* to the side to behold the Cross/Icon of Jesus—*you have been Called.* It was by that vision he had been called—some 5 years ago, and it was this Calling, which had held him to toe the line, creating his Spiritual Journals (for what other purpose then small monies, had yet to be revealed). The whole cathedral was smoky—from earlier service. T rushed to the site of his vision. He was *hungry.* Hungry for God. Then a *voice*—of Charles Shipley, Verger— called him back to the vestry to begin setting up for the Ceremony.

Now sitting in the vestry; before-stage jitters.

Sewing robes, donning robes; vestments, sashes; taking off street clothes.

PPM
Nada.

Sunday, March 31
Tho I'm not yet 70 years old, am thinking about Old Age Disability & Death. So tired.

Halleluiah, Halleluiah!

All the people filling up the church the OM had prayed about –to increase church attendance—are there! He is almost crowded out of his place!

Some of the regulars complain about the crazy overpacked 11AM service, and are astounded @ our oversize 6PM.

PM
Did I say, was thanked by very many people for my reading of Dry Bones—both after the Great Vigil last nite, and tonite, @ the 6PM.

Monday, April 1,
Had to shove Asian out of my way getting on the subway train. Stood beside 3 others in front and a group in back on the platform—train

pulling in, suddenly out of the side a slim older Asian female glides up to the door, cutting everybody else off but T walked straight in front of the clever person & w/his shoulder blocked her back to the side from whence she came. AHHH! She exclaimed. He entered w/the others who had also been standing there first.

Huge blax homeless man paces train, tan skin and nice but unkempt curl hair; he carries a plastic sack of belongings, another plastic sack tied to his waist. Dark-stained clothes.

He crazy.

Just when I almost getting decent amount to live that kind of a shock to somebody's income.

Have to pay to look @ naked bodies. City declared it illegal to go naked---as God created us. So the old gay men—and some young good looking ones—can no longer be seen in their nude skin, featuring their dick/balls—many shaved—not encumbered by any clothes other then shoes.

Nude flesh. It was such a welcome and relaxing sight.

But for $15 can go see naked men at the Nob Hill Cinima.

Street is decayed, Van Ness & Market; scruffy people in wheel chairs. Raged homeless man lays out on the sidewalk.

People of a low status; chatter in Espanish.

The sun was so hot he burned.

Parade of people went past going up/down; some of the very old creep out of their pitiful hovels on walkers straight into café to watch TV on Internet—not talk to others. Sick and on medication, locked in a world in their heads.

Baking.

Faces look so grey, poor, grimy. Living in SRO hotels, & depressed by it. Hotels where difficult to wash in the common shower, and no bath, unless you want to bleach it out each time.

Sun is out & all types of folk—the good, & the toxic.

PM
One story after another I hear, so cruel, old lady artist (photographer) first met @ Seniors is being fined for having an insurance policy worth $3,000 to burry herself with. SSI--aid to disabled— found out about it, and is making her pay a monthly fine for several months, so they are trying to kill her too.

Now my own story is added to it—and the sorry part is, none of us have anything! We are poor! We have so little! Yet the government agencies hound us!

It is impossible to live in this very expensive city on the guidelines they set! And we deserve to stay in the city where we have lived and worked a lifetime!

Red Jordan Arobateau
Tuesday, April 9, 2013
12-Midnight, Pacific Standard Time
San Francisco, CA

Part- 3

Tuesday, April 2,
All stuff out of pockets; belt, flash drive, keys, all coins, metal detector scan @ Social Security office. Per instructions of my case worker—*all will go well;* assures the Lord(ess).

Now he was waiting to hear his name mispronounced:

Red Rabtas... Red Rabtoas... Red?

There it was!

U$A's Social Security system began in Britain in the 1930's—most industrial advanced nations in the world have it, plus National Health Care.

Was sent to Medical office—Human Services, 5 blocks away.

Interviewed by pleasant Chinese woman; was very interested to know he was an artist; OM assumed she was Chinese—as she completely looked—and asked her: *do you speak Cantonese? No, Tagala.* How guilty the OM felt after saying such horrid things after the court case re: rude persons living above him (documented) hoping their island would sink into the sea! The lady cooed over him like a mother hen, and testified how: *I read, really read, and read anything I can get my hands on: I also read ebooks*—so he warned her his material was GLBT predominantly: *that's OK! I read anything!*

Coyote.

Sat in sun w/Old Jolly—his first comment re: a passing male: *I want him in bed w/the lights off.*

Sun hot.

Colder wind blows, faster now.

101

Tall heels parade themselves down Polk Strassa, tallest heels in The Life; women shapely forms and extremely well dressed. –No doubt they be hi-end hos.

Now here comes another very well dressed lady, older—the Upper Nob Hill Panhandler. Red full length coat, black tights, tall leather boots—thigh high— immense grey rabbit fur hat, far bigger then her head; big as a mushroom over a mouse, or a very large parasol—she wears $2,000 worth of clothes, smile on her face of a secret she has. –Which is this deceptive disguise of wealth, when she is flat broke & a beggar.

The wind was blowing & he was gone.

When he got to the Hos, the sun had gone out behind white foggy cloud; re-appeared, then faded, then reappeared—sun shone—a yellow hole in the white/blue sky—billowing blue; some fog. Then subsumed into coldness.

Blax fellow traveler sits outside on a Ho's bench, wears shorts in this weather; writes on a notebook w/blue lined paper. A mad writer!

Its cold now.

Cigarettes—life shortening.

PM
Nada.

Wednesday, April 3
One of greatest escape techniques of those who feel squashed, feel self obliterated, disappearing entirely; is to build up a grandiose ego— a super persona.

This is why some outrageous transsexual women are so hated.

On his wei, TM encountered a group of white men just exiting some yuppie venture capital business and foolishly they stopped in front of it blocking the sidewalk & gabbing their obnoxious kkkapatilist ideas of building their yup empires—steadily the OM was approaching then

102

he walked directly into them impacting several—who all jumped aside; OM continued on his way causally as a person would brush a fly off their arm—this is what he thought of their world.

Saw the lovely Rosa Salazar—as attractive as usual. Her tan Latin face, sparkling blue eyes, golden hair. We spoke of some of the agencies transfolks predominate in, funded directly or indirectly by our Federal Government fear of HIV/AIDS, and how HIV vaccine is in clinical trials—and a cure is about 1 year away. The government knows this & is already cutting back on help-funds.

Then did much today & must realize am in the service of the Most High—closer to Her-Him, thankfully, & more is yet to come.

The OM baked in the hot sun.

Red-hot heat bored into his bones.

I am back @ Mexican restaurant. Baz bought us a fish taco plate w/refritos.

Annie called. To Safeway again.

Annie is irate about the robbery the health care system is doing to me—she thinks:

> I think they might be devil worshipers—no I really mean it. Its not just money they worship, its worse then that. Devil worshipers. I am really mad they are stealing $104 from you because you are poor and have no money. They are devil worshipers—they probably sacrifice babies.

PM
I sit here in bare feet, trousers, sweatshirt, cap, in my darkened studio room, while Mr. Wayne dances naked for $ from the gay men next door.

He is leaving town, not to return, to PU work in the Catering industry in So Cal. I went into the theatre & left my biz card & a note saying if he ever comes back to SF to give me a call & we can have coffee. If he investigates the card, he will see my trans status.

103

So briefly the wrap up— my efforts to obtain sufficient monies to live, pay for Penny Cat's medicine & super abundance of food due to her illness— finickity appetite, has pushed me $45 over the government limit—so they are taking $104.90 out of my Social Security check in the month of May. *They punish you*—the government agency said this, themselves.

So, I have to hide the money. I have to begin by immediately hiding one of the direct deposit checks—and the second thing is to draw back on Bancroft shipments, so as to decrease those monies. —I can spend the extra time when not cranking out back-to-back shipments, by editing ebooks—so this will be productive. Also by resuming painting. Will have to live frugally—but will do one rent boy deal every 2 months just to keep *my hand in*. Uhhemm.

Thursday, April 4
The font of despair.

Native American Dental Clinic. I am in the system!

Yeah!

I would be a hero. TM thought.

All the ninos running around w/black hair; squealing-shrieking.

That TV priest show really stepped up to the plate w/woman's issue about a girl's rape in high school—good handling of the subject.

Crack hag squats on curb, filthy muddy gutter, between bumpers of 2 cars; her sunken in teeth; cigarette smoke balloons out of her wild head.

Transman laughs—laughs not in ridicule no; the woman—fallen, she is our world. Our nation's lionized greats, all those damn rich trust fund babies working to keep up w/each other it is them down in this gutter w/their fancy suits—they have generated her—they have given birth to her—it is them!

Day grows cold outside Coyote. OM put on his warm hat w/earflaps; waiting for Dr. Sam.

Drizzle begins @ Coyote.

The Lord has assured me re: my debts. Soon to see Dr. Sam & child—then eats! Yum!

The old gay man testified:

> He has a mushroom head—the shaft is plump—big, then flares out in a mushroom. Big tall guy like him you'd think he'd be long & skinny—no, short, fat & a big mushroom head….

Another old guy said: *I gave him $30, then saw him out in the street today he asked me to loan him $10. I said, no, I don't do that.*

You'll never get it back.

T remembered his adventures w/street trade in 1970—then he had not conferred w/other tricks—they didn't hang out, all but one or two. Now the gay gays hang out here, cruising the avenue; & we all talk about our trade.

Cold. Rain in the air.

PM
The font of despair.

One after another all the checks, direct deposit I've worked so hard to get, come in—and each will drive me over the top of the limit, $45 over the limit—fine $104, for the month. And I cannot barely live now!

I must hide this money somehow!

Friday, April 5

Mad hell.

Mad hell.

Cut off of Medical, then chineee—(Mandarin speaking) politely puts me back on again! Thank God.

Then go to buy a meal—find out I've been cut off foodstmps too!

Race down to foodstamp office; brother black puts me back on, he informs me —*it takes 7 to 12 days to process.*

Thank God.

All in one day.

Running crazy.

Explanation:

> I was cut off Medical for earning $45 above my limit—and cut off of foodstamps for not providing the Amazon receipt—my bank statement worked.

The burdens we carry—even a small dog who can no longer greet humans w/wagging tail; who can barely follow its owner, still carries it's weight.

Selfishness of people can be seen in Laundromat-- there are only 2 baskets but women there calmly monopolize a basket slowly folding clothes out of it—when others need it to transport wet laundry from washer to dryer. They could put their dry clothes on counter and fold from there—no. Selfish.

PM
Famed opera singer Maria Legeitte:—*she indulged herself in every possible pleasure—and died at age of 28; no doubt she was exhausted.*

The Old Man had taken the vow of semi-poverty, but had no community to share with. Monks and priests and nuns who dwell in poverty all live in community; they share food, housing, prayer; they are not alone in their challenges.

106

Saturday, April 6
I am cared for. Grace. Annie listened to TM's hideous problems, which surround OM like a wheel within a wheel—.

As an artist you can't estimate your hourly worth—only supplies—or you'll find you're sell a painting working for 25 cents an hour.

Fields bookstore bookstore closed. Last one down on Polk Street. I have lived thru the closing of these bookstores:

> Live Oak books,
> Jubilation books
> Babylon Falling
> Borders books
> Books INC
> Fields books

Only one of these was replaced—by an Opera Plaza bookstore.

PM
Prayers are like supplies put up on the shelves of God's storehouse.

Oh, a funny:

> There was this old lady who had gone senile—she was about 85. She had worked as a domestic all her life, for rich people; one by one they had passed on, and many of them had endowed her w/their fortunes, because they hated and loathed their families & hated and loathed their children, so they gave her all their money— and the SPCA, and their religious institutions. Also, while she was working for them they had taught her how to play the stock market—which was how they made themselves richer then rich. So the old lady was loaded; but a scam artist had taken her to the cleaners for $30,000, and then again for more money---till he had robbed her of nearly $100,000. The old lady had no family but her friends got wind of the scheme and soon a court-appointed conservator was given her care. He handled all her money and her affairs scrupulously, and went over checking on her every few weeks to make sure her house was in order and she was ok. He checked her phone and blocked the scam artist from being able to

107

speak to her. However a few months later, the conservator found to his dismay that the scam artist was back in touch w/the rich old lady and scamming her out of money once more. He immediately blocked the scammer's calls, and established a new phone number for the old lady. About a week or so later, the attentive conservator found the scam artist again had found out the old ladies phone number! He changed it immediately—but yet again, awhile later the scam artist had once more discovered her number and was continuing to scam her on the phone. The determined conservator set to work with an investigator and then found out the means the clever scam artist had to discover the old ladies number over and over! *The old lady herself was giving the scam artist her number!* It seams whenever the conservator changed her number she got on the phone to give all her friends her new number—and she'd call the scam artist and give him the number too! She missed his calls! She enjoyed speaking w/the scam artist! Somehow this tale was resolved to the benefit of the old lady who is so rich she did not miss a dime!

So much to report I can't keep track—I must go to Bancroft once per month now—turning in no more then $200 worth of goods---if I go my usual 2 months and get $400, it all comes in @ once it makes the fools in the system assume I'm making $400 per month which throws me over the limit.

Also, Grace operative loaned me $40, so I will survive until food stamps resume. I must be more frugal and my monitor money carefully so that I don't go over the limit—it is crazy! A thief would do much better! It is an honest person who gets caught because they don't know what they are doing!

Luckily young lady reinstated me in the free Medical program, and young man restarted my foodstamps—takes 7 to 12 days for them to resume, and Grace operative loaned me $40 to tide me over until then—added money to my bus card to get to Bancroft, called Bonnie and will see her next Thursday, with not many books—so as to keep within Medical's limit! And also must pay for Xeroxing these newly created JOURNEY journals (LIFE AT THE BOTTOM OF THE WORLD).

I love being @ Grace—when we are having fun, service, food, learning classes there. And of course my visions of Jesus, the divine;

and the Holy Spirit communicating a word, a phrase, an idea to me every now and then is cementing me in.

Great Googa Mooga!

Sunday, April 7, 2PM
Assemblage for the 90th anniversary of St Cyprians. Rev Will Scott priest. Kathryn Jeffers Shorie, Presiding Bishop of America in assembly—haven't seen her for 2 years. The congregants assemble. Tonite including St Cyprian congregation.

Many black seniors, life-attendees of St. Cyprians, fill the choir loft pews.

I inhabit my privileged position in Grace as person of color-- of which they have few.

The mighty organ begins.

Bright eyes of the choir. Exuberant in their song!

After service, the OM looked around the massive nave, near the labyrinth—people were scattered here/there; some working @ churchly duties.

I won't interfere between God & His/Her lambs.

Finally realized I'm no greater then any of these motherfuckers—but I can do more.

He could do more w/his gifts he was given.

God I want a prayer that is going to be answered.

People walk around in white robes—are not wicked, they are good—a doctrine which is good, is what they study. Compassion, love, mercy.

We spoke of Christians doubting themselves, --as to their relationship to God/Jesus; we don't need proof. Most of us need solace, comfort for ourselves; closeness to Christ.

Bad incident when coming home—saw a group of 6 people, mostly men going into my apartment, I came in behind them, just in time to almost catch the door but one of the men turns & slams it in my face!

The OM pounded on the door ferociously hollering: *YOU MOTHER FUCKER!*

Immediately the young woman w/them turned & hurriedly went down the steps, opening the door for OM: *you remember me, I saw you in the hallway that day we were moving in*—said the young woman— she was light skinned African American w/curly hair: *Yes, I remember you, trying to move that big heavy sofa.* As the old man angrily stomped down the hall leaving the 6 young mostly all white privilege assholes assembled by the elevator the idiot who had slammed the door on him was apologizing, his words floated along the corridor: *I'M SORRY SIR, I'M SORRY SIR,* but OM did not dignify his lame apology w/a response.

He had been typecasted. He had been rejected. He had been judged by the color of his skin, his manner, his age. He had gone to the door carrying a cane, limping, with packages and had had his own door slammed in his face—after paying nearly $100,000 dollars rent over the last 11 years—by a young fool.

Vengeance is Mine, says the Lord.

I think the bad thing about this shit is it installs fear in me—that I am part of a dying breed—the poor of SF. Those who, regardless we have lived & worked in the area for 46 years are on a slippery toehold trying to stay. Who are outnumbered by the young—the young & mean, but primarily the young & uncaring.

The fear that I will have to go, eventually forced out, by poverty—and where will I go? Where can an artist be but in a big major metropolis—and where can an Oldster go but to remain around a small circle of friends/colleagues the have assembled over half a century!

Have had young students slam the door on my face quite a few times—and hope some of them get killed. There, I've said it.

Monday, April 8
Sleep. God has washed my soul clean.

A frantic crack-addict runs thru the downtown streets on a mission, digging into every garbage receptacle. Recycles cans for coins for crank, no, wild white man, he looks more like Heroin.

First for the family. —Re: prayer requests of clergy, parishioners. You go first to the church family. —Those who have been serving you communion, those who have been gossiping w/you over coffee in the dining room—Those precious lambs!

Some homeless wandering along as if they'd found an alternative world w/all the physical stuff provided free w/out working— similarities of the real world—a pack of them seated at a closed restaurant's table, chairs, chained up in front. Or who set up a tent on the doorstep of a private dwelling.

The problem is it is not so.

Met another young man, lets all him Adam—have heard his name tossed around for months. Attractive youth:

> He has a nice piece of meat, he's sexy in bed—but he's too needy; bugs me after sex—he sees you in the street, follows you around asking: *can you give me 2 dollars?* Or he asks: *are you ready to have sex again?* I'm old, I told him, I don't have sex every day!

Well if you can't be good be careful!

Joe is over at The Jolly Olde Pervert's:

> Just dropped him off down the street, he's probably sucking her off right now.

@ yupster taverns across the way, the artist wears barrette, Persian style. He has begun work on the other panel—standing on his step-ladder.

111

Soaked in sun. Old Jolly up street probably being sucked off by Joe—or he sucking off Joe?

Hot sun. All people out.

Must mention lady w/cat I tried to help is bugging me—there's nothing I can do for her—she is not my responsibly, I only did the little I could—but she is crazy which complicates the whole deal:

> Can't you talk to them for me! Did you see them and talk to them for me?
>
> It won't do you any good, I can talk to them but they can't tell me anything about you, because of confidentiality! You have to go up there yourself!
>
> Well wait a minute will you!
>
> I have to go! I got stuff to do myself!
>
> Cant you at least call them!
>
> You should call them! Call them; even better go there in person!

I may stop trying to help people—its nearly impossible. Will wait to see how this turns out.

Cracked out humans walk past—on illegal medication.

People w/their dogs one hand on leash & little sacks of poop in the other.

Have seen the unhappy faces of people being forced out of their apartments.

They have worked—but not enough to compete w/the super rich. No way.

PM
Nada.

More & more our nation is espousing familiar socialist rhetoric—the field of social welfare—national health care, public schools, governmental housing projects; yes, it is not the dreaded communist plot. It is the basic facts of human social welfare. Housing, jobs, food, education, medical coverage! —Those who preach hardcore socialism entirely are not popular. This is because preaching a doctrine is like a cook who makes a stew w/salt—salt & nothing else. Salt is to be added to flavor the stew.

Re: Small capitalists –single, privately owned business: Fidel Castro banned all small shops and private enterprises—as Kapitalistic. However they are beginning to resurge in Cuba. It was a mistake to ban small mom/pop businesses. They should be controlled only if they reach megalithic proportions, or, when the time to inherit comes to pass accumulated wealth down to an heir. There is a difference between petty Capitalism, and hideous octopus tentacle strangle-hold price-fixing Korporate KKKapitalism.

For all the gifts of healing one has—& closeness w/the Eternal it remains the works of justice—that are calling to be done all over this earth, for peoples. It's selfish greed corrupting the planet—which needs to be addressed.

Good! Those Wikkileaks revealed our governments cover-up of our meddling in foreign nations, endorsing & backing corrupt dictators while publicly endorsing 'human rights' & democracy—when in fact U$A endorsed leaders who were tyrants, dictators,—Pinochet—Chili, the junta's in Spain.

Tuesday, April 9
Beware the happiness but at somebody else's emptiness.

OM discovered he'd sold 2 hardcover books from Lulu—but thru Amazon—in EU: HOW'S MARS, and LAY LADY LAY. So the giant has hooked me up! Thank God! Its such a strain having to send out those books myself! Finding them in my stacks, worse having to assemble them page by page; packaging, wrapping; waiting in line @ Post Office.

113

Coyote. 2 of the other older gay men speak of their work lives—they are lifers; they are still employed; one wears an attractive watch—for 30 years service; the other directed asbestos removal @ a facility. There were 8 departments—all of them had men dying of asbestosis's —but his. Because he followed the recommended protocol; —gloves, encasing materials w/barriers, bags, etc. He had no deaths from asbestosis's in his unit. Meanwhile in the other units men were going to the hospital dying. His men would be completely suited, and wearing their respirators—gloves, and all materials housed in plastic sheathing or bags. He'd look in on the other departments, those workers would have taken off their respirators and were ripping out ducts and pipes made of asbestos w/their bare hands.

One guy said how he was in the military for a while and the bosses came in—the brass—checking for gays:

    Any gays in this unit?

    Oh no!

And he's gay and half the unit were gay also!

Well as you know some of the people who I was dealing with in my youth—who I was so thrilled by, so enamored of—now come to view w/distaste—or avoid—for my own protection.

The penitentiary is bigger then all the men are; they go in young, strong, & stupid; & the pen beats them, whips them—every single one.

A tranny girl walks past—hate to see her so shredded & diced; cropped lips, jaw, nose shaved to crisp point like a pencil; clipped eyebrows shaved replaced by red lines—her hips padded, flared out wide, gigantic, — by silicon pumping; likewise her large breasts. (Yum.) A cigarette dangles from her mouth. Alas, she is moribund; but going out in style.

My gawd!

WAHHHHHHHAAAAAH!

The most horrible screeching ever heard—a woman wheeling a tiny baby in a carriage. Baby crying its fool head off:

What happened?

He didn't get a ball.

The horrible screech continues down the street and up the hill---all over a ball.

A Hos employee sits eating his lunch on a parking lot bench. When done, remain 2 large treys of packaging, now garbage. He politely takes this garbage to dispose of them in the Hos cheap-ass tightfisted garbage receptacles! They won't fit!

HA HA HA HA HA HA HA!

Then the employee politely attempts to sit the garbage atop the wretched garbage receptacle —but, since its rounded, the garbage slides off down to the pavement, HA HA HA HA HA HA!

This is the problem the cheap Hoes has got for being so afraid that a few starving recyclers would reach their grimy hands inside searching for recyclables that they built the deposit holes too small!

HA HA HA HA HA HA HA HA!

The poor we have w/us always.

Heard gossip from one of the processional of tenants who have attempted to make a go of a certain store—the one that formerly housed our beloved BABYLON FALLING bookstore.

When it was clear the tenant could no longer afford to stay in business, they had to escape their lease—but the greedy wench who owns the building (won't say what nationality for fear of offending my Chinee friends, but *they know... they know...*) anyway she refused to cut the tenant a deal so they had to ante up huge sums to escape their cruel lease—and as they handed over their last check the vile landlord offered them a job as *a building manager*. What an insult.

Well, the Australian shop will be no more. It too is leaving— however a year remains on the lease, so what to do?

> There is no logic in this! The twisting...
> --Overheard, street

Proud pugs parading.

Came down street, saw lovely young girl-boy who was in my play (INHABITANTS OF A GHETTOIZED POPULATION)—she has gone all the way masculine—still as a girl! Blond hair in a crew cut, soft bosom under satin man shirt & tie, curved hips in male trousers, & men shoes—looks completely androg!

> I worked in the oilfield when it went belly up. It went belly up, folded up and was gone in 30 days. People don't believe it could happen that fast but it does.

Want to see this happen to this Silicon Valley; very very greedy.

There's boom then there's bust. Everytime there's a boom, then there's a bust. Waiting for the bust to this greedy Silicon Valley computer hell to go bust!

Must mention the Pot Pies:

> Annie Ho kindly informed me her grandmother had purchased 25 Chicken Pot Pies for her—and she'd put them in her freezer and eaten none of them.—That was 7 years ago. Hearing the OM was out of $, foodstamps; she kindly drove them over to his house in 2 sacks. The OM ate Chicken Pot Pies exclusively 4 days, until they ran out. They were not spoiled. Were nutritious and hardy—and tasted like cardboard.

Wednesday, April 10
Day break; the sun plummets upward in red.

Am @ Coyote—5 old gay men seated outside. Younger Cosmo speeds up/down Polk Strassa wildly between 2 pieces of trade. We sit on lawn chairs in the sun.

Evidentially one of his youth trade called him a fat bitch. & stomped off down the street. Promptly the gentleman went off after him— trying to woo him back.

The Owner comes by hands on hip, campy, sardonic expression:

> You looking for prostitutes –they're down there on the corner—

All laugh.

Sun beats down like all the other cities of street life—New York, Chicago, LA, Oakland, SF.

Car drives slow past, handsome young man looks @ me long & hard. Everybody thinks I'm a rich gentleman. Painter across the way pressing on w/his artistry on the other panel tables & chairs painted on this one. He is a slow careful painter.

My God I'm getting cruised from everywhere!

Spring has sprung!

The blood is running! The mating urge is upon all human & animal flesh (and bird and fish & plant).

Overhear the following conversation:

> Depends on where he died—on hardwood floor? Or a rug—it keeps the stink in.

> Old guy, 76. he died alone.

> I went to the floor under his, smelled like tar. Roofing tar—but nobody's roofing in the neighborhood. I went up to his unit, outside the door smelled an odor I've never smelled before.

Sent a repairman out—he found the old guy—dead.

Gigantic jet blax crow wings its way across street—rushing traffic below.

PM
Must tell you there is a world of difference in how upstairs neighbors* are behaving; a lot of quiet—precious peace.
*--The rude, ignorant & thoughtless peasants.

Thursday, April 11
Squirrels race about—play in the greenery.

Bonnie Bearden informs me about Restricted Access. As you recall a friend of mine whom lived in commune w/in the early 1970's spent time w/the Black Panthers in those days—I did not, spending my time instead in the dike bars, gay action groups & women's small groups & Lib marches. Joan saw & heard many things, including the inside tale of the murder of George Jackson inside Soledad penitentiary—for which the affluent son, lawyer Steve Bingham had to go underground 25 years for fear of being falsely convicted of conspiracy in that matter. Joan thinks she knows who the real culprit is—someone who has gone on to obtain a high position in the prison system—and she wants to write a book about it—an exposè. We agreed if she sets her barre to high—this dream of writing a whole book, which will be a best seller— she may procrastinate and never write it. It is suggested:

> Why doesn't she just start w/an essay, encapsulating all the facts, dates, names, what happened. It's quite a daunting task to set about writing a whole book—if you aren't particularly a writer.

> Well could she put it into the archives—and if she's gets cold feet upon releasing it publicly—they could hold it...

> We could put it into Restricted Access. Nobody can open it until the date the person sets. A lot of people set that date upon their death.

Birds twitter.

Sun blazing down UC Berkeley campus; sound of wide-open space. Smells of greenery:

> Such a beautiful campus. You know it was designed that way from the beginning. It was designed to resemble the Ivy League campuses of back East. Mrs. Stanford, and Mrs. Bancroft were friends, close friends. Both their husbands were filthy rich — their husbands had no use for education or high ideas, but their wives were adamant about supporting the educational system and it was Mrs. Bancroft who designed and laid out the UC Berkeley campus — Mrs. Stanford, the Stanford campus down in Palo Alto.
> --Avraham

Wind howled outside subway tunnel as the train raced back to Civic Center from 16th & Mission—the OM had overshot his stop—again— having first gotten on the wrong train down in Berkeley!

Re life; he tired & hungry & disappointed. Tho a smile on his face

Saw the public library: *My books are in there.*

You have made culture.

Seagulls shriek in air circling. Beautiful hot sun baking him. OM be soon $230 richer.

Beautiful hot yellow sun. Blue skies.

Huge dome of Civic Center—City Hall towers overhead like an octopus—scary.

Well this truly proves to me pigeons can see 3/4th way around their heads –small heads w/beady orange eyes facing forward—I threw crumbs down almost behind its back—but Pigeon spied it and came running over on its red feet.

Am seated in the sun, it soon will leave. Mild breeze blows— harbinger of cold to follow.

Very pleased am selling books.

The trans lesbian watercolorist wasn't very friendly. If there was a vacant chair by nearby you, she would not sit in it & join you, no, she'd calmly sweep it up—along w/table, in a muscular grip— & then walk off w/them down to the end of the store frontage to sit isolated, painting her blue, green, orange, yellow, red, watercolors; seemingly content to be alone.

All those Job Cards pasted on deserted Gone-Out-Of Biz shops on Polk Street. They signify carpentry/pluming/electrical work to be done—when the owner gets enough money. Some never do.

Well, as you know, every artist wants their works to be known & appreciated; they might confuse being read & sales. When first found people were stealing my books I was pleased—*they really like them!* –Tho I got no money from this.

Saw his friend Old Man Syd cross Ho's parking lot—age 85—& wondered casually: *what keeps him alive?* What kept Red himself alive—so much desire to do my work—to see the fruits of those labors--& to manifest works undone! *What keeps them alive?* While others let go @ 40, 50…

The OM going home. Sound of cooing in his mind.

We are cold and hungry please help!
--Cardboard sign in gutter w/tire track run over it

PM

Too hard to achieve in our society even to own a home of ones own or afford their child a college education. Not just the rich who always get there, but for example one who achieves under all circumstances can also, but they are very unique; because few can overcome all these obstacles. The rich will point @ these extra-ordinary achievers and claim every poor family also can succeed—but this is myth. All help must be given the poor to work towards success. Average persons who are not as smart still can achieve and can have clean, prosperous, and a civilized life.

But what makes these rich, criminal, is the hold which they have over our lives.

North Korea making nuclear weapons & selling them to the rest of the world. Their weapons now within range of Japan & US ally Guam.

I know I'm doing less harm to the world being a poet, then making nuclear weapons.

Friday, April 12
Trolley stop @ Castro-Market, how boring. No more nudity.

No more skin bare, showing all!

Comancho & Kensey Lamb called; going for food, but am on my way to clinic for blood draw, will see them later.

Prehistoric mammal tusks are being hacked out of ice, sold for ivory. National Geographic magazine. Thank God they are dead—eons ago. Asians continue the modern day elephant tusk sales—murdering off thousands of elephants. It is a dirty, sad business.

We must begin elephant ranges in other lands the callous Ivory profiteers can't get their hands on.

Read also about the resurrection of prehistoric beasts, thru DNA cloning. To be placed in Jurassic epoch parks.

A stupid idiot runs in front of the trolley car on the tracks. He gets on the trolley, the driver tells him how stupid he is. Then the fool begins a rant about being mixed race, and having brothers: *darker then you* (pointing to a dark skin woman) and others white: *I'm never going to be white, I don't think. Whites don't accept me.* The fool complains. And complains how he is disabled and grew up poor—everything he says I have lived, others have lived and there is nothing exceptional about his ass—plus it was him who got his self drunk; loud jackass.

SF; only town w/4 seasons—all in one day.

PM
Must carefully monitor monies. Can't earn too much on paper, or will be thrown off my medical benefits & foodstamps; nor too little as cannot live.

Now to edit LIFE @ BOTTOM WORLD –2, for Bancroft funds, and POD Text hardcopy; it is Volume 18 of my JOURNEY journal series—will #20 bring a breakthrough?

One thing; these rich people in these rich TV house programs will never know a day in their lives they are calling the foodstamp office to see if their food cards have been activated.

I can't believe a person never worked a day in their lives. Well, it is true. Tho hard to fathom. Somewhere in life someone has offered you a job—a friend will call: *come on w/me quick, their hiring down @ Ace Department store—inventory, for 2 days. It easy, all you do is stand there counting things, and they're hiring anybody they can get,* so before you know it, there you stand getting a neck ache, your feet hurt, you are tired, bored, in a state of torture—but you go the distance until they send you home for the day and call you back the next day and you work the torture once more; get green cash money and some co-worker there tells you about the next place they are hiring, duefully you go along, and so you have entered into a work life—but this man, he never had worked a day in his life—and he's bisexual, and a communist.

Well Comancho is in town, treated me to a delicious lunch—the OM was ravenous. Comancho is getting success on his website—but T was not suppose to divulge any of this. However, the OM was impressed.

> God: What do they say I Am?

> Red: They say You are dead. They say You don't exist.

Saturday, April 13
Meeting Comancho & Kensey Lamb; food. Out food gathering.

After devouring half a sandwich, the OM spoke w/the 3-some— including their lesbian friend from New York City, who also just married her wife. Sold some postcards for a few bucks—it is good my works are wanted; my name spread around.

Wonderful time in sun along the venue. Talked about parenting. The many ways all my queer friends are having babies:

> Ovary harvesting
> Surrogates
> Artificial insemination
> Fertility drugs

Oh heard the name mentioned; Valarie Solanas, today... That odd gal, panhandler, hustler... Playwright.

Program about Satanoya—life living in harmony w/nature--Japanese. Nature preserves where storks –big Cranes—are brought back into existence.

An insect larva becomes a butterfly. Goes from an infant to an adult in 1 hour.

The Catholic Church torturous inflexibility derailed the lives of millions of people. Yet still another case—of an infertile couple, whose Catholicism forbids the use of sperm donors, surrogate mothers, artificial insemination. They will go childless all their lives.

PM
Glorious day w/Comancho/Lamb; Baz; older gay men @ Coyote. Fun.

Am impressed my friend Comancho is very good friends w/J, a lesbian who just had a marriage to her woman. They may have children in a while.

Sunday, April 14

> Going to church is an act of presenting yourself to God—every week.
> --Rev Jude Harmon, from the lesson.

The idea that once upon a time, way back when, when the church was @ peace and everybody got along—is not true!

We see from Paul's letters to the Corinthians and the church in Ephesus all the discord and problems which were going on there. Mad helluva lot problems! Debates over dietary restrictions of the Jews, of which comprised most of the Christian church @ that time; also circumcision. Also amount of good works they were or were not doing!

Many people simply go to church, hear the service then they leave. You go further—you come to all the groups and there you hear all the dirty linen aired.

The Spirit enunciated to him—the fountain geysered white spume 4' high, so thick he could eat it. And the Spirit is real—tangible—not simply words in Torah, but acts of flesh and substance.

All camera people out on the plaza made T nervous. He felt he was a target—deer caught in the headlights.

Nervous. Paranoid.

It is hard for a Christian to grow up & realize the church is not all about they themselves; or their work, even; is not all about themselves; —*me, I,* —their work, the work of God; God has blessed the individual w/this work, put it in their hands to do & that work is from God—this is human author; the human maker of it; the human deliverer of it; they are the vessel the physical source & *not the end in themselves.*

T had noticed he was a persona—as he set in the sun—at least 4 people spoke to him—they knew him! Some by name & they were only vaguely familiar to him. One said: *thank you for your presentation the other night!* (At the Great Vigil.)

No Annie. He went home alone.

PM
Oh. Did I mention, got a thank you on YOU TUBE for my multi-racial video. These are always encouraging. The brother stated: *you I need to do more of them.*

The Growing Wisdom. —Title for next JOURNEY Journal?

Monday, April 15
Its difficult looking into the face of privilege; young, white, skinny, affluent, & they don't have a clue.

OM felt like wrapping his cane around their faces—it would bring repercussions, but it would be worth it. He felt it would be worth it.

2 killed, Boston Marathon—bombs exploding.

Then he spotted pale green paper… ran to it brandishing his cane ready to spear the paper.

Wow! Found a $5 bill in the street.

Next; a handful of coins in gutter! Quarters, dimes, pennies!

PM

> One thing we have learned from history, so many things are forgotten, history is tenuous, so easily forgotten.
> --Huell Howser, California's Gold

This is why I am writing my stories! So they will not be forgotten!

I must say I am delighted by my work.

Tuesday, April 16
Found, 1 dime.

Saw African American student type man, he walked about 40 feet in front of me. Saw something fall out of his pocket. When the OM got near that spot, he saw a crumpled paper—he raced to it. It appeared to be a $10 bill! OM bent down, quickly pocketed the bill. The man had disappeared into a building.

Awhile up the road, after speaking w/several he knew:

> Old Man Syd: 85
> Young Rachel: 22

He went into his pocket to unfold the bill & stick it in his wallet. It was a $20! <u>Yeah!</u> Money for small foods & to do his laundry!

Coyote. Its empty (of gays).

Henny & (Old) Adam, were down @ tavern visiting a very nice, handsome, bartender who just started working there who they knew from a fine gay club which changed hands & turned straight…

All my friends are busy.

Wonder what happened to A? Not @ church; did not return my call.

Several of the old guys drifted past. T privately wondered what they knew about him—he figured they were beginning to find out. But when they spoke of their prostates, or sexual dysfunction due to old age, it was a bit embarrassing, knowing he had different set of mechanics to work with.

Old Jolly came around. We sat & talked:

> Look that that one over there, he will. —That one in the red jacket.
>
> Oh no! he's not my type.
>
> Why not? He's breathing!

Realize how much trouble it aroused; listening to too-cool jazz; shooting drugs—pain deep seated—how much have avoided it & am sustained by faith in Jesus Christ—.

PM
If you are a real artist you will have less time to study, read. A true scholar must read, learn; this takes time. So you might not master as much learning as a scholar.

> We are given elite status in culture so as to aid those who do not have elite status.
> --Program on Bonhofer, World War 2 Nazi resister.

126

God says I want you to go up to the state & cause it to be a legitimate state, not a criminal state.

In Hitler's time, few dared to stand up to his illegal dictatorship— those who did, they were called the Resistance. Some of them, who dared, died in concentration camps. Both Gentile, & Jew.

> Have you read the instructions manual? --The bible?
> --Eric Metaxas

How many places on earth its illegal to talk about religion.

> He (Bonhofer) didn't lead his life as if he wanted a long life—he did not say I want to live to 80—I want to make it to 90. He died @ 39.
> --Shirley Hoogstra, TV

Wednesday, April 17
Smell of new building materials.

Shrink.

Coyote.

A queen saunters by w/her male boyfriend; queen or TG? Angular shoulders. 6'6" height; stylish but poor clothes; expensive boots.

Saw the handsome hustler –Joe—he stalked by; attractive, rugged, beard stubble, black hair; teeshirt w/older man w/dog on leash— somewhat TG form; his latest date?

> Hey Joe!

> Hey!

He wiggled fingers @ the OM—at end of muscular white arm.

Somebody runs afoul of the food stamp law—not reporting their measly little $60—& foodstamp officials take them to court, stomp all over them—but the people who make the laws & then help themselves to the whole pie—they can't be caught, because they've engineered the law.

The people can see what's real & what isn't. We know the powerful change laws, adjust them so the whole funnel of wealth is tipped towards them, and even if the law allows them—the people know it is an unjust law, a corrupt law, a law, which should be disobeyed by civil disobedience!

Merely make a change in the law and pull down a half-million dollar salary per year.

Case recently small town CA, top 4 officials were taken to court because over the years they'd raised their salaries to over $750,000 per year for the mayor, $500,000 respectively for the vice mayor, and the sheriff. The town was only 50,000 people! They went to jail for fraud.

Saw his reflection—magnificent man! He was a perfect picture of robust, broad-shoulder stocky, tan skin oldster w/big fat gut.

PM
354 --?; for --?. THE COLLECTED POETRY OF RED JORDAN AROBATEAU—1.

People have no idea what its like to be an artist. Some go to work in a factory, restaurant, hospital, office; but an artist has to find their own studio—and pay for it.

An artist must spend their own money on tools they will use. It is not furnished for them, as the employer of a factory or office.

Some go to work for others—at a job designed by other people; they work and get pay awarded by the amount of hours they labor. The artist must spend their own money on supplies, then work—for no pay unless they sell a painting or a novel. Above all, they must invent their product. They must envision that painting. The theme of the book; it is not pre-designated for them to do by someone else!

Thursday, April 18
OM sat in street w/coffee he afforded. It is early afternoon—going to fun event @ Grace—Evensong service & food @ reception.

128

When he was young & mentally ill—he could have died by the wayside, but did not. Fell into, then out of drugs quickly. Had let go his drinking of firewater.

He remembered the desperation of those years the slow smoldering angst, desire; fear & trembling.

Hot sunny—he climbed the hill. The cool somber stone walls of Grace. *Catha*--dral. Seat; of power.

Lawrence begins a beautiful organ passage.

The OM discovered he did a lot of praying in this short service. His heart was moved once again in that esteemed establishment. He cast up prayers for his beloved Penny. He prayed, and reached out to touch the Almighty. His mind followed the service, so by their lead he also gave thanks to God(ess) which frankly was something he hardly never did.

Later @ the reception—OM devoured a lot of hor d'oeuveres. He spoke w/Annie & Wayne; and Denis—the 50-year member. And said hello to others he did not know as well. Priest Mark was there also— he had delivered a meaningful dresh which he showed Red later was from the writings of someone, on Jesus' message in Mathew:

> Be happy if you are homeless, poor, because you are near to God. God is with you.
> Be very sad if you are rich, because the rich are far from the Kingdom of Heaven.

In the reception dined on foods—then thank you's for the volunteers @ the homeless hotels was made, and the OM was pissed his name wasn't mentioned—tho he had actually been a volunteer there, one of the longest, over 2 to 3 years (as documented in JOURNEY journals). The praise went to the managers—and this, he recalled, had bugged him from the very inception of the program—when a manager had been chosen—not from the stalwart volunteers like himself (who for many weeks had dragged out heavy tables & chairs by himself, alone; having arrived earlier then any other volunteers); no, but a white upper middleclass volunteer—whom obviously they trust more, however this is a mistake in society. To always glorify and entrust these people, while continuing to step on, and use, and overlook the lower ones. In the long run this creates a very negative affect.

So there, you see the first sentiments I felt, upon finding a manager had been appointed over us, back @ the hotel, (circa 2009) instead of me, who had done so much work—and inevitably it was a white educated upper middle if not upper class male. However that man is now dead.

PM

Well so much has gone on these last few days I can't begin to say—in the news. The U$ had been troubled about the pig-ruler of North Korea starting a nuclear war—suddenly this has been far overshadowed by domestic hell of our own.

The Boston Marathon—a runner's race, which is very old, established— was the site of a double bombing in which 3 were killed and 175 people injured—many severely; bloody, human body parts scattered all over, w/countless amputations needed. Just a day later a massive fertilizer factory explodes leveling the town of West, in Texas; then 3 shootings—killings in separate sites within Massachusetts.

It appears to look like some kind of activists might have done the double bombing, in Massachusetts—because of their youth. It is incredible how our CIA captured pictures of the bombers—out of a sea of thousands of people—w/legible faces.

Biggest electronic dragnet FBI in history.

Can't believe it!! Turn on TV 2am, 1st suspect in Boston marathon bombing has been not only found but killed! 2nd is on the loose! Suburbs of Boston shut down. Citizens told to stay inside. Bus, subway shut. Urging all business to shut! Second officer shot & killed. 2-cars carjacked. Convenience store robbed. High-speed chase—where gun battle ensues, explosives thrown out of fleeing suspects car litter the freeway; that's when 1st suspect killed!

It was a rapidly moving story. FBI put out pictures of suspects.

Step by step had rolled into place; right after police issued photos to the news-- the suspects showed themselves.—Then the chase was on!

By then our CIA knew who they were—from the Russia Caucuses— Chechnya nationals, but raised in the U$. They had been bright, award-winning students in our American Universities.

Now the hunt was on to capture the 2nd suspect.

Massachusetts county around Boston & suburbs cut out bus, subway; police flooded the area from surrounding cities and towns, flying in from all parts of the nation; police surround the town convening to trap the suspect.

Bring in all the resources available from the state, surrounding states, & across the nation. Officers from all jurisdictions; Sheriff department, Highway Patrol, City, Federal forces.

All humans are a part of society—even social misfits on the outskirts; outcasts—they are a part of human society.

Boston now locked down. All residents told to stay inside. Buses, subways businesses closed. People going home to wait; search for the second armed suspect killer, begun.

I must tell you privately that many I've spoke to were hoping it was not an Arab doing this bombing—not some Islamic jihad—and we were reassured by the white-skinned individuals in the photos—very American in style— that they were just home grown fools; however sadly this is not the case. They are from a nationality whose religion is Islamic —and a land very acquainted w/the Jihad hatred terrorisms seen on TV.

A little sperm-producing male walked down the street; he was hot in the crotch, shabby bearded face. Innocent face kid. To think the 2nd killer—no doubt schooled by his older brother to participate in this carnage, was just like this—age 19, now his life is over.

Basically we all want same things—creature comfort; food, water, security, warmth, its only when people get power that their tastes become more refined.

Friday, April 19
People have God for solace--& call on Her/Him in times of great struggle—or disasters—others go further with God in their daily lives, to do some kind of service around God. It is some special work—or *Calling*. This is not necessarily higher or better or more superior then the others—it only goes further; & these must be, by this framework, closer to the Eternal for they are calling upon, and seeking or in service on a daily basis.

Suddenly they were gone. Gone. No Suburban Utility Vehicles in the neighborhood. Fancy furniture tossed out in a hurry, laying in the street.—That was the death of the dot.com boom, a scant 11 years ago.

Boom then crash. Boom, then bust.

PM
Talked w/very interesting gentleman—an older gay crony, 75; he lived in Germany, and was a child during the end of World War 2. He saw people blown up by bombs. The average, simple German civilian's gladdest day was when the Americans came marching in, liberating them from their fake Nazi dictator.

Have a small confession to make—am so goddamn tired, BARS ACROSS HEAVEN was ordered by Amazon weeks ago, and am still procrastinating to paste on it's ISBN, wrap it and have it ready to ship @ Post Office. This is another book which must be OCR converted as soon as possible!

(And save me so much damn trouble what w/the assembling, wrapping, mailing…)

Saturday, April 20
Liquid must be let out thru the lower body parts. Or there will be leakage. Some of us oldsters might leak—when we can't get to a toilet in due time.

Guess what I am a human being & I don't care!

The older OM got, the more human he found himself to be!

Not so worried about his public image. Nor so self-conscious!

An unpleasant incident happened in the Wal-Grims. Picked up a roll of clear mailing tape (to wrap BARS) which was on sale—so it appeared— @ $6 for 2 rolls, or $2.10 for a single roll. W/that, and other items went up to counter. When the nice clerk rang up the bill it was very high. In amazement asked for her to itemize it. She had charged me $6 for the single small roll of tape! I explained it was on sale—but she foreign speaking) could not quite grasp the situation. The manager came over; a stodgy, short, older Chinese. He shook his head—*no, no*—and showed me the tag—w/his thumb covering the $2.10 price. I calmly peeled his thumb back revealing the $2.10 price. A third party witness (white) came over and said that the sign was conflicting: *this is false advertising!* I declared. And fussed and fumed, how I should call up the general headquarters, and the old Chinese was huffing and puffing demanding $6—for shit. He indicated to the others they must remove all these signs from the display! –In an almost frantic tone.

Your manager is an idiot. OM declared to the two young Chinese— the nice clerk and a lower level manager (a handsome, intelligent & much more modern appearing lad). They could not reply for fear of their jobs. They gave me the roll for the $2.10, which it plainly said on their advertisement.

Made mental note not to buy larger line items in WalGrims, without throughally checking first!

And also he remembered it's the same store which cheated the Wicked Witch of the West—sidekick to the Evil Hawk—cheated him out of $60! But sadly, the Witch did not confront them, & let it go by, thus robbing himself. –Most doubt due to his genteel upbringing.

As OM proceeded across the street, a pretty, older Trans girl, brown skin, came over to him:

You were in that movie Transgender Tuesday weren't you?

Yes!

So was I. I'm glad you called that man out. A lot of my friends have had to call him out—they cheat in there.

He is an old stubborn, mean, cheap, stupid Chinese, and dishonest. And he is an embarrassment to Chinese people everywhere.

Especially the new wave of people—educated ones.

It is a sorry truth, but people like him who are stupid, stubborn and cheaters, manage to make their way up to the top of the ranks in many facilities, --hospitals, factories, offices, government agencies, post offices; because of having no imagination, little intelligence, hence nothing better to do w/their lives, they aim to go on & on in a tired, stodgy, bureaucratic position & rule like a queen on the throne. Alas, because of union seniority, they cannot be removed. Have seen this w/white, black, in the olden days. Some old mean employees had gone into work faithfully 40 years, thus advancing themselves up the ladder to promotion, but slowly loosing their cognitive abilities over time/boredom—while coinciding get more & more mean—and become a cesspool of trouble no customer would ever wish to run afoul of.

People walk past of all ethnicities, all types—all attitudes; every expression etched on different faces—but the unexpressed pain which most are able to hide well—the silent scream.

An ancient relic of a man, hands shaky, totters over to a bench on the parklett—part of the jungle outside Coyote Café—smoking. Blue cigarette smoke. His toothless mouth hangs open—he dawdles. Shaky hands put the smoking cigarette up to his lips again again, repeatedly.

Diana Ross, the Supremes—

You keep me hanging on.
You don't care a thing about me—you're just using me.

134

Go on, go on, get out of my life,
  & let me sleep at night
You don't really love me,
    you just keep me
  hanging on.
  --Motown, circa 1961

Music of jubilation.

1958. Outlaw kids, gay, in restaurant booth, jukebox, 4AM after gay bar closed.

Some victims of Boston Marathon bombing must have 2nd amputation on top of the first emergency amputations. In hospital.

270 total injured in Boston bombing.

So he had already done battle that day w/forces of injustice—just by going to the wretched WalGrims of dishonesty!

WallGrims trying to charge me $6 for a tiny roll of tape! Didn't the clerk notice something strange about that?

Their inflated prices, their bait & switch techniques.

When he was not working the OM may have thought he was wasting his young life sitting, a wallflower, to the side of the tavern observing the gay fun crowd; rarely a participant; seldom lionized; & observed he felt the same these days, that he was wasting the last of his old life—most recently here @ Coyote—however he was part of a festive chit-chat group now, outside with the old gay men.

    That's a hot mess thar'! Shit fuck!
    --Wired wild white Okey gal in parklett

Across street was filling up w/the privileged Yups—

Extremely muscular younger man—must have served time in jail—& there had nothing to do but work out w/weights, acrobatics; he's crazy—able to jump to top of parking meter—and stand on it! his 2 gymshoed feet on the tiny head of the meter.

135

Young Yups are amusing themselves across the way.

Wind is picking up.

See the he-witch w/his purse, fringed w/ostrich plumes, colored crimson; Sara Cohen, is the purse's name; sauntering around the corner—too bad; broken pal-ships; a world in disarray.

Rowdy level PU across street; (real) woman w/very loud deep voice, bellows, cackles, talks in a stage volume built to project to the outer further reaches of a theatre.

Blax bro man way clean in casual clothes & white girlfriend pull up in his sleek car, go on in, he is part of security for the evening.

A woman asks man:

     Are you already circumcised?

Here in this part of town, in this city, in this nation all are free to be couples—lesbian, interracial, gay, trans. Everyone. —If you can find somebody.

The OM had spoken casually to about 7 people he knew—briefly—only for a few minutes; had spent this much of the day more or less alone.

Rhythm, jazz, pop; TM reveled in the background music.

Mild wind blew. --- Rhythm plays; he prepared himself to move towards leaving.

Now wind blows continually—harbinger of the cold evening falling.

A beautiful pigeon soared into the air; grey soft fathered belly up, triumphantly turning into the brilliant sun.

Rejoice!

Church tomorrow.

Well, Sat nite this week was done & maybe he'd see his friends next week---& enjoy them like a long drink of cool water.

For now he had his books & painting & felt he might be working against time, eventually removed by the rich city & wanted to get as much stuff on digital as he could. —So as to be like a traveling salesman carrying his goods in a carpet bag on his back.

Pardon me sir this is the handbaskets line only.

I wish you'd leave town! OM was momentarily furious yelled! Stupid white young clerk.

He stared deeply into their eyes. With so much terror in the TV news maybe his stare would have a chilling effect on them.

Pigeon hobbling along—but OM had no crumbs. He took out kernels of frozen corn, warmed them in the palm of his hand, and threw them down. The birds dined on the corn.

The skies have flying creature; bird's wings flapping, sailing, around.

OM saw a wallet-like item lying on the filthy sidewalk —rushed to it; opened it—empty; tossed it aside. He sat on fire hydrant to rest.

Blax man comes over & eagerly PU the wallet—thinking he'd found something—it was nothing.

They were all poor.

PM
Oh! Forgot to mention—saw old friend Napoli, the cook, @ the former Persian restaurant. —He is back @ the site, —now under new owner—moonlighting from his first job.

I am teaching what I have been taught.

Revolution is all around the place:

Information sent out to the public
Allies assembled
Radical people put into power where they
   can help affect justice & necessary change

As well as assemblage of actual fighting weapons.

Love is expensive.

Sunday, April 21, 2PM
Have gone without food most of late nite—morning—after meal of
ground beef, corn, beans, and greens—kale—shake. When head out
to church will get cheese. First cheese in days.

Did I tell you the ethers have shook down TV channel 9 for me, after
several years of blank screen—can now get this fine public channel!
Dinosaurs coming up Wednesday, Dust Bowl on Tuesday! Yeah!
Maybe there as a class action suit against Comcast or one of the
monolith kkkorporate entities who perhaps were blocking it so us
poor people would have to sacrifice to pay for their hi-priced cable
shit! Fuck the rich!

Transman wondered where he was going as he headed uphill to
Grace. Still had no girlfriend, still not famous. All the few things he
desired. OM had a date w/destiny—which had not yet been kept.

Grace class.

I know the truth; God says.

The priest leading the group asked God for our thoughts to be guided.

The low class struggle over dollars—stark survival; hunger. Where
to get food to eat? The middle class—angst over other things. Their
career. The meaning of life. But its 2 sides of the same coin.

We can react from fear—or from love. Same truth but from a
different place. They don't compete w/each other. They exist right
on top of each other.
----From the class, Andy Loban.

138

From the very first experiences; his adolescent awareness of the church, its image of had been corrupted.

Andy thought that the image of the church, its all the same, the corruption, peoples bad experiences in the church when they were growing up—in the street--& there it is discarded; they want nothing to do with it. But the raw center of the church—people of the triune (trinity) love, we carry the faith.

> Cathedrals are big places that have pillars you can hide behind.
> --Kevin Holdsworth Bishop of Canterbury

OM had spent the weekend essentially alone & that unhappiness sat down into the bottom of his guts.

Spoke about community lacking people in your home to help bind up your wounds.

We talked about this cloud of life. Some restart their lives thru all the clouds.

> Sometimes the curtain breaks open for only a moment & we see eternity; we see heaven.
> --From Andy Loban

When these breakthroughs occur puts us in more free access, over on the other side, the heavenly side.

Again the worship area is vast—white marble stone spread out the width of the nave, sweeping from the grand entry doors and up to the last rows of the pews. Too few chairs—by design.

Some congregation sits. Some stand.

My God! We're still in Easter! I thought that was a month ago! Its getting me confused!

No hanging out w/Annie again this Sunday.

Ah! Something wonderful & delightful about the Ho's—their planters, about 4 feet high, filed w/green grasses, sit in saucers—can catch the water—birds are able to drink from them!

SCORE!

Oh, PS, what a lousy weekend.

Saw friend inside; together the 2 waited in line in their shabby clothes, carrying baskets of too few purchases shared their anger @ the Yups.

Well I must really tell my shrink how I am not the only one who experiences rage inside the grocery store---my friend, the other day, so enraged @ rising prices, our one-room studio apartment homes in jeopardy.

This gentleman is *catless*, because of being too poor to afford senior animal care costs:

> I have always had a couple of cats, as long as I can remember—but I can't anymore, & it's a drag man; too expensive. I'm catless.

On his way home OM spied an old man in a wheelchair begging:

> 6 months! 6 more months till December, I'll be 65.

 Then he will begin Social Security and medical benefits.

This system has provided dignity for people—not seen prior to the 1930's –who back then lived in the shadows of their relatives, often abused, neglected, underfed.

PM
499 ! from -!. COLLECTED POETRY- 1.

Love must be given everywhere.

All God's creatures they want to be loved! The small kitten. An unwanted child. An oldster. Aren't they all made in God's image, & by God's loving Hand?

The stand looking out from their portraits in time exclaiming—*I am wonderful! Why aren't I loved? I deserve to be loved!*

Saw a great program on TV—(the new channel 9, wow so much good stuff ((PBS))—about a hoard of nuns, w/mother superior and sisters— all of them a collective nunnery midwife service, w/one doctor, a priest. The latest episode a deformed child is born and the key factor is will the mother suddenly bond w/her little child, who loves her so much—after early weeks of rejection—at the daunting task of caring for a child who is deformed and will die after a short number of years.

Monday, April 22
Saw Veronica, young tranny gal. Intelligent. Bright eyed. Me & her & Bro Baz must all get together again soon.

Pleasant talk w/some of the old gay men; one has been diagnosed w/cancer & I have prayed for him in the collective church prayer, & will pray again.

3 of the guys discuss prostate/bladder issues; of course I am a bit challenged by that issue, but have never been personally questioned. I don't know how many of them if any know my transsexual status!

I've said this before; cops are a two edge sword. They are hired to keep the peace. And in so doing some commands they are given by superiors are unjust ones. The cops are sent out to evict destitute women w/children, to remove working-homeless w/no place to stay to rest before their job. A child dreams of being a Do Good Officer, loved by the public whose valiant deeds save many—but in reality s/he might be acting as near to a fascist as you can get in a free country. It all depends on the commanders above them, upon how the law is written & interpreted.

Today we encountered a gentleman of age, in the streets who had participated in the Harvey Milk riots back in the 1970's— as you know Dan White, a former supervisor, a former cop, had shot & killed

141

gay supervisor Harvey Milk, and the Mayor of the City of San Francisco, George Moscone—a decent man. He went to trial and was found guilty:

> When the verdict came out—the sentencing—and we saw Dan White was only getting 7 years for the murder of 2 people—one of them the Mayor of the city—we went wild! Milk was a hero to gay people, and he should not have died that way! We marched down to City Hall and began destroying it, and any police cars in our way. We set fire to the squad cars, and to the front of City Hall! When the fire engines came to put out the fire we threw chunks of concrete & bottles at them and they backed off and let it all burn! We uprooted parking meters from the street. I swung one of them babies @ a cop and down he went. We were taken to jail and I was transferred, and taken to hospital w/injuries. Can you believe, the cop I'd hit w/the parking meter was there right next to me, getting 23 stitches in his head! He was saying: *If I ever catch up w/the son of a bitch who hit me in the head, he's gonna pay for what he done to me--* but the truth is, I was sitting right next to him and he didn't recognize me! You bet I kept my mouth shut!

Some rotgut blaring blues issues out of Coyote; its suggestive of sexualization; didn't say so in the lyrics, those low-down rhythm and gravely tones will speak it in full.

Trouble-run 1950's ghetto, deep South Side Chicago in the blocks of the 30's, and 40's between State Street & the El.

Will the dreams of the homeland survive?

Beautiful pigeon soars thru air high, above 5th floor; smaller by its height in the sky distant; sails, wings up, V shape, teeters, changes directions on a wind current & descends, drops to roost on top of a neon streetlamp overlooking Ho's.

2 pigeons; grey, purple, green, velvet sheen feathers; beak w/white cere; one feeds the other; the thicker neck one feeds the smaller neck bird—a female? Or adult and adolescent? The smaller neck approaches the larger wanting to be fed again.

Saw D Young V on my roost outside Sushi Rikka. His building management job is way better then the old one—due to the fact @ the old place the boss was insane.

Also, no shows for awhile—not sure where he can show.

The last several people who have had shows at a certain art gallery, have all been robbed of their monetary proceeds by the gangster dealer. He a hustlah. No Good.

> A certain lady artist we all know took the crook to court because of not receiving her money from sales of a lot of her paintings—close to $10,000. She got a lawyer. She won the case. But all the court could do was put a lien on hustler's bank accounts—and by then he'd taken all the money out of them. To date she still has not been paid. We artists not only put heart & soul into the creation of works, we also put money for supplies and sacrifice time taken off of regular wage jobs—in order to produce. When we get little back in return it has a horrible effect. It breaks the wallet. It defeats all but the toughest spirit.
> --Red in conversation

When you work all your life to create a product, it is hard to keep self-respect when the world places so little value upon it.

PM
Green/White—out on my shoulders; first time in month or more. Been so stressed. They sit on the same shoulder (Bijou's, —the left) —preening each other. Reunited @ long last.

FREAK! FREAK! My god the girl in this love/sex poem I'm just now editing—written 45 years ago? The girl is just 15! Aurrrgghhh! (SCRATCH OUT THE CHOICE.)

Tuesday, April 23
Everytime I think that: *ah, I got nothing to do this Tuesday…* I remember the FTM group—sadly think of it as something toxic & I don't want to risk going to.

The sun is my best friend these days.

Seeking the golden, hot rays beating down, warming me. Sitting out in it—on lawn chairs in front of Coyote, on fire hydrants, ledges.

Where we are born onto this earth we are born into a tangled web—of human society. People want to make money off of you, by your labor; if you are in jail the prison gets government money for you as a statistic, to line their pockets; if you are laying comatose in a nursing home, the owner of the home collets money per head, per bed. People make $ off of you when you die, embalming your body or burning it up. Yuh can't escape it!

PM
Brief program on the female/male birth disparities in India— these proud strong women of India are fighting sex-selection. Sex selection laws are on the books, activists have worked for this 20 years, but only *one* case has been prosecuted. Sex selection abortions are routine, in the hundreds of thousands, aborting female fetuses—most doctors do it. The practice is more prevalent all across India today then in the past with the rising standard of living families become more prosperous so they are able to afford sex selection.

The deck has been stacked against India's females from antiquity. The set-up that only the male can carry the family name. The practice of female dowry.

Stable middle class don't care—if they have 2 girls and one boy or 2 boys and one girl. Or even 3 healthy girls. It is those struggling to climb up to the middle class who are concerned.

Oh one last detail to add to this day—in which I struggled to remain holistic, exercise, socialize, and sun-ize—was coming out to Cosmo:

> Well you know Joe doesn't like to do but just a certain types of things in bed... how was he with you?
>
> Well I have to tell you, I don't know if you know this but I'm transgendered. Transsexual
>
> Oh! I didn't know that!
>
> Yes.

Well that means you were a woman and now you're a man!

Well sort of both, actually.

In all honesty, I made it seem like I had been born a hermaphrodite—which may be the case in a mental-biological way, tho not a biological-of-the-flesh way. It is so much easier. Because they always question: *so you were a woman and now you're a man!* When you know you were never a woman! This is why you have pushed yourself so far back into the direction your body should have taken, when it was being formed in vetro!

Joe lost his room. Suppose to be in it for 3 months.

He was bringing women in from the street. You know all the street girls are crazy for him.

Then we found out there was a condition to the penal system giving him the free hotel room for 3 months—

He got kicked out because they gave him the free room to begin with --that he go to training classes and narcotics counseling. And he fucked up; he did not go. So now he's out in the street.

Yeah he's out there and complaining. *Oh woe is me, I can't do anything right. The world is against me. I'm so depressed I want to die.*

Wednesday, April 24
Thank God—Foodstamps did come in—only $37—but it's saving my life!

So the essentials of OM's life * revolve like a mobile and must be kept running in clock-work order. One thing after another break down must be readjusted, a part taken out, replaced, every piece of it must be observed @ all times. Now the food stamps part is broke, must be fixed. Cannot let it break my spirit—but I'm fighting it & continue on w/my work.

*--Medical benefits
Food Stamps

145

Church aid
Bancroft funds
Amazon monies
Senior discounts on PGE

Butcher paper in window, another boutique goes out of biz:

> Goodbye SF 5 years 3 months ago we began our store. We cannot
> any longer afford to rent here.
> --Moving out sign

100,000 years ago humans begin spreading out from Africa.

Many same sex male couples go past hand in hand.

There goes a friend. You can't help but love N. with her prettied up
fancy clothes, her power, her lawyers; she is an heiress and also
works for a living; she is self-assured in dealing w/the world and will
take no shit. Empowered 1st world woman. She will not be moved —
because of having an excess of wealth.

> When de communists came dey took all de teachers away— den
> dey took de people who waz a little bit smart, who tried to help de
> people—dey took dem away, den dey took de priests away. Den
> dey tore down pews und statues out of de church und smashed de
> alters & turned it into a dance hall.
> --On Russia in the 1920's revolution.

The Old Man gave thanks to God. He sat outside Coyote; the passel
of old gay cronies had just left. Saw motorcycles ride by; he could
have lost his life driving on highways 100 miles-per-hour on the
backs of motorcycles in 1960--in a flaming wreck.

And not just by the angst of a 20-year-old transman's young life's
emotional pain, & childhood abuse mental repercussions, but in a
explosive flaming steel concrete red-blood wreck!

A pigeon took off like a shot, flapping hard.

The sun returns brilliantly---warm @ Ho's—small dog's pink tongues
lapping. Bright rays.

Piercing siren of yet another ambulance roars by in a red/silver streak.

Small dogs gallop across the intersection on their leashes.

PM
200-million years ago Tumasic period. Dinosaurs began.

Each species endures its disasters. It is theorized a gigantic space
body—a meteor—from outer space crashed into the earth kicking up
dust clouds which blocked the sun, for years, maybe a decade, killing
much of its vegetation and starved off all larger mammals.

50 million years ago; like all Empires, the reign of the dinosaurs
comes to an end.

As far as these Yuppie rich taking over the world's big cities, driving
out the poor, the old:

> *Boom then bust*. Remember.

For everything there is a season.

Thursday, April 25
Grant Writing Center—1 sale only, 2 loan—of my books. Aurgh…
My ship still has not come in!

I can see the distant shores—flapping wings; white robbed figures
circling towards me in clouds.

Is this the onset of old age, when the Other Side begins to break thru?
When we are assured that life does not end stone cold dead in a coffin
like all the funerals a child has witnessed—but there is the beginning
of a new life springing up—beyond river Jordan, beyond the pale, just
beyond human sight.

***

*When the last homeless are removed you're going to see the darkness
come upon San Francisco.*

It was about this time the TM began to realize he was in the middle of it, witnessing the progression in escalating form—the raising up & reality of a very large fascism machine. And he was stuck in it---like those who fought to survive during World War 2—fascists rolled over their native land all they can do was wait for change to turn again in favor of human life; & in the meantime, the in-between time, take his NOTES & paint a picture or 2. An archeologist coming back upon these works will find they are a digesta of his era, his struggle— comparative to many odd people's trials @ the same time—but theirs mostly unwritten.

Red Jordan Arobateau
Friday, April 26, 2013
1AM, Pacific Standard Time
San Francisco, CA

www.ingramcontent.com/pod-product-compliance
Lightning Source LLC
Chambersburg PA
CBHW020443290526
45785CB00002B/984